1

I will dispense of the Oscar performance of saying Thank you to all the uncounted names. Thank you to all the generous and kind people that I encountered through my life and who made this book possible. Thank You! "Kukorachik"

Chapter 1
My Childhood

Sitting in a sunroom on a barrier island in North Carolina gazing at my own reflection in the glass, shadowy and mysterious even to myself. A face, round, and slightly pudgy from age and too rich diet of damn good food. Unfortunately the cook to blame is I. My skills in the kitchen bring me lots of praise and thanks, and I must say, well deserved. Conceited devil.

I was born in Ebenau a German village in Southeastern Poland, an area known as Galizia. This Galizia produced some very hardy type of people, very independent, freedom loving, self-assured, opinionated, and always with open arms to their fellow man. Their doors were never closed to strangers. All this happens to this unique person, described above, born in the morning, 10:30 am, May 25th 1932, according to mean spirited sister, who had to sweep the barnyard for my arrival, no less. So What! She was seven years old.
(*Note: See sketch of Ebenau at back of book*).

As the 10th member of the family of Katharina and Johann Hupert. To be born in the same house as the rest of the family and delivered by a mid-wife of uncertain talents, who also dabbled in witchcraft. Since the people of this region were a superstitious lot, of a mix of Ukrainians, Poles, Germans, and Jews. I don't know what superstition rite was called for the birth of a boy. Probably at least a birch twig broom by the front door to the house which was spit on by each visitor to ward off bad spirits. They named the not so wonder boy Adam, who everybody called Adamchek, a Polonization of my name, and I was told because of my cuteness, I became the darling of my older sisters, and especially to the Ukrainian maid who became me and my younger sister's Nanny.

The Family consisted of the following living members: Anna #3, Johann#4, Maria #5, Hedy #6, Rosa # 7, and joseph #9, me #10, and Helen #11. #1 and #2 died in the war between the Bolsheviks and Poland in 1919. They were named Anna and Johann. #8 was named Joseph who died 2 weeks after his birth. This area of Eastern Galizia was continuously being disputed between these two adversaries, in both the past and future times. An artillery shell loaded with poisonous gas, hit the house. It killed all the livestock and the two first born named Anna and Johan. Their names would not be forgotten. Father's mother, a widow, also died. Father suffered severe gas poisoning and had to undergo a primitive cure of being confined to a room of smoldering damp straw to make him cough. He survived and lived to the ripe old age of 86. They all were hiding in an earth cellar in the yard.

The village where I was born was founded by German Immigrants in 1792, which they named Ebenau, near the Town of Grodek Yagolanski, close to the provincial capital of Lvov. At the time of my arrival, the Village consisted of one street, lined with about 30 houses. 12 were still Germans: the rest were Poles and Ukrainians, mixed about half and half. This area of Galizia was dotted with lots of German founded villages, way over 100. Some still retained their German origin to the point of school and church services being held in German. Especially in the villages founded by Lutherans and Mennonites. The Catholics were easier to Polonize because of their common religion.

But not always. Villages founded by more than one religion were also easily absorbed by the Poles. This Polonization started well back the century before my birth. Overall a real homogenization was in progress between the ethnic groups of Poles, Ukrainians, germans. The 4th group of the mix of people were orthodox Jews, with a quite large presence mainly in towns adding more color to the rainbow of humanity.

The occasional Romanian gypsies tracking across our territory bringing with them excitement and intrigue. The contribution of the German immigrants to the native people was immense and lasting. It was evident in better homes and farming methods, majority of their descendants were better to do than their neighbors. The same time everybody had something to learn and contribute from their culture to everybody's benefit food clothing holidays and uncounted little everyday things.

My parents decided to quit farming the year I was born. The reason was my father's experiment with artificial fertilizer, it made his crops grow and bear fruit in abundance also prolong the gestation period with disastrous consequences, the crops could not be harvested in time because still growing and got caught by seasonal rains, just to rot in the fields.

Father was a complex example of a man, this multi cultural area produced. He was a more extreme product in many ways, confident in his own righteousness the same time very generous to his friends and neighbors with loyalty not to be broken, even with the threat to his own well being.

While farming, they employed a slew of five to six field hands male and female. Mostly live-in who were part of the daily routine from breakfast till suppertime. Sleeping in the hayloft where their morals were not highest and the sex abuse quite common, without any consequences, to the man. In today's world they would be arrested and tried for rape included my father, their attitude was their entitlement.

My mother would exchange her house duties for the maid's field work, so she could get away from the many kids and the confinement of the house. Mother was of the same stock in as many ways as my father. But few of her own uniqueness, very religious in a practical way, not condemning sinners to hell, "hell" I actually never heard her refer to just forgiveness of our sins and salvation because of our repenting them.

She always had a smile in her face that was replaced on rare occasion by pure fire in her eyes brought on by some injustice not to her liking or moral conviction. The maids in exchange were flattered by the change of status and everybody was happy. My mother never lost her love of the outdoors, to the last of her living days.

My father was the only boy of 4 kids, as His father had died when he was at the age of 8. His mother leased their land out and eked a meager life for the family. My mother was the 2nd child in her family of 2 girls and 1 boy. Her father died at her age of 7 and her mother got remarried to a local farmer and they had 1 girl of their own. My parents got married in 1912 and had a premarriage agreement for my mother to receive some acreage from her mother in law, what was to come handy in the future.

In the house was spoken 3 languages, German, Polish, and Ukrainian; Polish predominately. Father was from a catholic family, mother from a mixed catholic Mennonites. Grandma wore dark clothes with no buttons just toggles and loops, on her head typical Ukrainian babushka style covering, a cloth square in design and folded into a triangle tied under her chin and always black. She lived with grandfather in the village with her youngest daughter and her family, consisting of husband and

2 daughters. Grandma was quite strict and would discipline us kids and make us behave, she also had an earth cellar in her room accessible thru a trap door where she cultured some of the best "yogurt", which she gave as a reward for good behavior and in summer wearing a shirt, around her was a must. Since my sister Helen and I romped around barchester in summertime, very much to her dislike.

Father decided in a new career purchasing a small dairy plant operation. He began making butter, cream cheese, sour cream, fresh cream, fresh milk, and cottage cheese. The plant consisted of 2 rooms in an apartment building on the ground floor, the building was located in the corner of the town plaza, 1 room for production, and one for retail sales, which was my oldest sister Annie's domain including the bookkeeping. Oldest brother and one maid were the sole production crew with occasional help for wrapping the butter that they produced and formed into sellable sizes. He also collected raw milk and cream, on 2 days of the wk with one horse drawn wagon. Occasionally father would do that chore.

The cream and milk were collected from 1 farmer in different villages, who was in charge of a milk separator provided by my father. Local farmers would twice a day bringing the freshly harvested milk to said farmer for processing in the milk separator and we buy then the cream only, they were paid by the quart of raw milk and its fat content which was checked twice in a month on any day selected by my father, this was done to prevent people from adding water to the milk. If anybody got caught then they were paid on the lower fat content of the milk for the whole month. This twice daily trip by the farmers was looked forward to and appreciated. They met other farmers to exchange gossip and ideas and whatever happened in their daily lives and to plan social affairs for the village, something like the store gathering in the American west. You have to realize the only communication was on meetings and word of mouth, no phone, except occasional messenger fitted with a clapper to announce his presence to read his message a very rare occasion.

Most of the production was sold wholesale in a nearby big town Lvov, for that he had 2 independent salesmen, one a Pole named Urban, and for the gentiles, and one named Jacob for the Jewish brethren. Jacob was a very imposing figure in his high black boots wrinkled and always dusty, grey pants, black coat and hat, his face was surrounded by a majestic beard. He appeared to us small kids to be 10 feet tall. Later in my life I always thought him to be St Christopher incarnated. Just imagine him carrying baby Jesus on his shoulder, no problem at all. One time he bought me and Sister Helen an ice cream cone what a treat. And the only one for that year.

With the purchase of the plant we moved into the town of Grodeck from one place to another back to the farm house that was not yet sold. In one of the rentals know as "Hapkas" with a big yard with few out buildings, mother always has to have some geese, ducks, and naturally chicken for the eggs she needed in large quantities In time we also owned a big Hungarian sheep dog, a beautiful bitch which in time had puppies which were very much desired by the farmers.

On one occasion in this house my older sister Annie was instructed to dress me and Helen for church which she detested and let her anger out on me and sister's legs. While she was putting on the cotton socks she would be pinching our legs only to cease on our squealing and mother's tone of displeasure. I was not 3 yrs old yet.

Meanwhile my parents bought a lot with a small old house on it just 1 block away from the center of the town, the lot backed up on a 100 acre plus lake. They started to build an apartment house 3 stories high with a walk out basement apartment for us. The money from that project came from the prearranged marriage agreement. When getting married. The lot had very steep sides toward the water and the shore was not suitable for playing or swimming. For this we walked to the other side of the lake with the sandy white flat beaches, my age until 10, most kids' bathing suits were not required or for that matter not owned. My parents were I guess lower middle class. The same time every day clothes for playing after school activities had patches and most the time for me hand me downs. Hunger was unknown to us and food would not be wasted, and looked on with relevance, I give u an example, dropping a jam covered slice of bread on the ground it better be an accident we had to pick it up scrape off the jam and dirt and eat it or face physical punishment.

Talking about bread, which my mother baked most of the time, she loved to bake bread, no loaf was ever consumed without blessing making the sign of the cross with the knife on the bread and only then sliced for consumption, the bread was eaten fresh and up to 10 to 14 days old, each stage gave it a different flavor and use. In my mother's bread baking, she also baked a flatbread baked with white flour and topped it with sour cream sometimes with a locally made cheese, green onion and bits of bacon, I guess a thick crust "Pizza Pie".

One of the maids was to become my sister and my nanny and moved with us in one of our moves to town. In one of our many moves we landed in the farm house not yet sold, just mother and us 4 youngest kids. The farmhouse and stable were of new construction; the original got destroyed in 1919. Both buildings were masonry and covered with stucco or plaster, the roof was one third tile and the rest of straw thatch, I guess they ran out of money.

Insurance was not known commodity, the house and stall were attached to each other on two different levels, the house was 3 ft above the ground with steps leading to the entrance hall and the house. The

steps and floors were concrete. Also in the yard
was a very good size orchard with lots of fruits of
every variety native to this climate one of them
rhubarb, so this journey to the country had its
hidden rewards appreciated by everybody. On one
of the stays in the farmhouse I was enrolled in first
grade were I did poorly.

On the farm site we raised pigs and chicken only,
pigs were kept in a masonry built stall, that was
specifically built for that purpose and contained
pens for the pigs and a big boiling pot built into a
brick heart also a cooking and baking stove for
everyday use. Everything was wood fired and quite
cozy. On a big slaughter day 2 pigs were killed and
processed into sausage and other products of great
taste. That was done by professional butcher father
had hired for that purpose, most of this product was
sold by the salesman Urban in Lvov.

During the day of the slaughter of the pigs, while
they were hung up and cleaned and cooled down a
feast was prepared with great anticipation by
everybody. Fresh lard, lots of onions, garlic snips of
tenderloin, liver, kidney, salt and pepper, and lots of
sweet paprika on pigs brain everything eaten with
fresh baked sour dough bread. The aroma of that
feast cooking was to kill for, we were joined by
extended family members living in the village and
good neighbors especially Uncle Jacob, the
grownups on that occasion toasted vodka to each
other including the women, we kids used water
because soda was unknown in our house. On this

day my older siblings were not present because they were in school in town or working in the dairy plant so it was only us 4 younger ones, this fact was very much enjoyed by us.

On the farmhouse property there was a bell mounted on a wooden tower belonging to the village, sounded 3 times a day to indicate special hours of the day and on occasion for emergencies or danger, on one of the special occasions we had severe thunderstorms combined with hail pelting the village and growing crops in the fields, grandfather came running in pants and a course work shirt without a collar baldheaded to ring the bell in hope to appease god for deliverance from the catastrophe in the making. I still can see that little man ringing the bell with an up turned face and unshakeable trust in god's mercy a sight never to be forgotten.

That year there was a wedding in the village of a Ukrainian a well to do farmer's daughter. The bride and the groom arrived in the one street in the village from the Greek Orthodox Church from a nearby village sitting in a wood sited horse drawn wagon on bales of straw covered in blankets. They were followed by a couple more wagons with the immediate wedding party. Being received on the entry to the village by a boisterous group of young people eagerly awaiting the scattering of candy, cookies, and small coins from the wagons. This wedding lasted 2 days and ended with the arrest of few men for fighting. What a day.

While living in the village Brother Joseph tried to join the Boy Scouts and was refused because of his German Heritage. What a great disappointment for him. Discrimination was a way of life for us and never stopped us from our goal of moving forward. On that occasion I was made conscience of our status in the Polish society not understanding why, just a fact to live with and to experience in every country that I ever lived in. Not excluding the USA.

In the summer of 1938 after school closing we moved again to town into a house next to our lot with the apartment under construction. Living in town also brought on Polinization of our families to the degree no German was spoken in the house, also in our daily lives irregardless. Who we met in our daily travels, grandparents, uncles, and aunts, Polish was the language.

That year Christmas memories were made not to be forgotten. On Christmas eve we entered to the living room/dining to a Christmas tree lit with burning candles decorated with garlands of straw and different color paper chains made by our older sisters including some half dozen glass ornaments. Mangers set up on the base of the tree on straw that also covered the wooden floor of the room and set down for a grand meal of fried fish, 2 kinds of pierogies, followed by fruits, baked goodies and a compound made from prunes and dried pears. What was a must for Christmas Eve meal.

Singing and toasting followed the meal and opening of the presents, never more than two and some of the presents were meant to be shared, like balls, skies or sleds. We were interrupted by a group of caroling young people at the front door. They were showered with goodies from the table and toast from the bottle and some coins being passed on by my father with a generous hand, more for strangers than family.

Little did we know that this Christmas was the cultivation of hundreds or more of happenings and encounter of different people and their cultures and customs what a experience just to end in the near future in so much bitterness and wasted lives and destruction.

Living in town exposed me to some great experiences. There were special days of each week. Wednesday was market day, farmers would arrive with horse drawn wagons with wide variety of goodies to sell from home made butter, cottage cheese, to calves, piglets, chicken and every imaginable fowl that there is, fruits, vegetables, baked goods. Craftsman of every variety, shoemaker, toymakers, pots repairmen, knifes and scissor sharpeners and naturally pick pockets, Who if were caught got instant justice from the people around them with smacks, hits and a farewell kick in the behind, in front of the conceding gendarm.

The atmosphere was unbelievable the noise, dust, food vendors, and the smell from all the animals and some "humans". The gypsies were another seasonal happening in our daily lives, they arrived in their covered wagons and they were dusty brown canvas dreary type not the fancy Hollywood versions, late spring on the way from Romania to the Russian border with stops in the town. They camped out for a few days resting on the grounds of the animal stock market. At the same time trying to earn some money or barter for food for the horses and substance for themselves, palm reading or music playing were their biggest enterprise, it would not shrink away from day labor and mercy on any chicken or duck on the street. Later in fall they'd be back on their track to head home for the winter.

The gypsies appearance brought lots of superstition of the local people, to the surface some funny some sad. One of them involved my father, he found out that a Jewish Taylor was to open a shop, father showed up on opening day to be the first customer, knowing the Taylor superstition that he had to sell something to the first customer, my father conned the poor fellow into a custom made suit "English wool " for ½ price. English wool fabric seemed to be the highest of design in fabric, and if you could afford it, that fact gave you some status of some importance, you had arrived. It is not that he didn't have the money, just the thrill of winning the contest of wills, bragging rights about his English wool suit.

In that suit he went to a bank convention in Warsaw, in his homecoming he told us the story of him and other men thinking of being strong enough to lift a gold replicable of the bank of Poland headquarters building with one hand just to fail in disappointment, if the lift was accomplished the price was the said building. What he had to do there I do not know and he probably didn't either.

Winter time put a damper on most activities except midnight New Year's celebration of the Ukrainian, what was celebrated with a mass on a frozen lake on an altar made from ice. Quite a site to see all the lit candles everywhere in people's hands and on the altar, what an experience, together with the sound of prayers and cracking ice.

On 1939 began peacefully with normal daily activities, my parents were finishing the apartment building and renting it to prospective tenants, mostly junior officers of the Polish army, they never moved in . One feature in the yard was the coop for the chickens, geese and ducks that my mother insisted to have. Our apartment had another curiosity with a bread oven, just so my mother could continue her love of baking, bread, cakes, strudel, and other delicatessens, everything was wood fired typical for this area.

Chapter 2
The War Begins - 1939

With the war on the horizon, things started to change dramatically for the worse. The mobilization brought lots of crying and hand ringing, farmers had to turn in their horses and if they were found to be fit for the army, mustered into the needs they could fill. With the lightning fast advances of the German army, lots of mayhem and suffering was prevented against the Ukranian and German minorities, the same time the horses were liberated and recouped by their owners. At one occasion we 4 kids were at grandmas when the German attacked a nearby small military airport. With the bombs exploding, we were instructed to go to a field across the street and lay down between the potato rows for protections from possible gas attack what was in their mind, and I still remember this from the 1st world war.

We survived this attack with all the blusterous black smoke and to me it seemed like the end of the world with the ground shaking and loud explosions in the air. The start of the war also brought out old resentments between the Poles and Ukrainians with lots of suffering even death among them. The German troupes camped in the park in tents. On a foray by my brother Joe and me, were pointed out by some Polish boys as being Jews, the instant reaction of the soldiers was threatening and charged with danger, we left the camp in an accelerated speed coming home and told father about it. Who immediately went to the commanding officer in charge to complain with the result that we were treated with some cookies, candy, and a tour of the camp which we declined, I hope the Polish boys didn't return to the camp because their lives were in great danger.

After 3 wks the German troupes withdrew and with them father, Johan, Annie, and Mary, in a horse drawn covered wagon which carried bails of English wool cloth! Given to my father for safekeeping by a Jewish merchant. Mother the nanny and sister Hedy, Rosa, Helen, and Brother Joe and me stayed behind to witness the Russians enter the town, I almost forgot my father's small dog a wonderful animal also saw the Russian triumph.

At that time in history the Bolsheviks and Nazis were buddy buddy, the Russians garrised a platoon of soldiers in the apartment, we were led by a junior officer, a handsome young man always in immaculate uniform. The women were all a gaga and full of adoration for that man. The soldiers themselves were very friendly and lots of fun, in the evenings when they returned from duty posts there was instantaneous storytelling, singing and dancing from some of the soldiers from the caucus area of Russia. I also learned a Russian ditty and can recite it to this day.

The Russian authorities came to our place looking for the goods the merchant had entrusted to my father and had declared them their government property. Now I don't know was my father a thief or caretaker. I guess both.

Chapter 3
Forced Resettlement 1940

In early 1940 a German resettling commission arrived to sign up the German for transport to Germany, what most Germans did including us. The Ukrainian nanny became a distant relative of us named Anna Hubert, a name she retained to the end of her life in 2009. Mother took a dangerous chance with that action, if found out, she would have been harshly rewarded by the Russians and Germans alike.

We went by train to a camp by Berlin in Germany a place called Kirchheim. In this camp the Nazis found out what obstinate and stubborn as a mule, people they were getting lots of friction from both sides. Me and Sister Helen were hauled from the train station to the camp in a car. A first for both of us, on top of suitcases and bags, laying down for that ride. This Ride would not be forgotten and for that matter not desired. The camp was for processing and resettling only, we were joined by father and settled after a few weeks of extended stay in former western Poland, this part being Germanized. Most of the delay was called by Sister Rosa's acute appendicitis, after her recovery we went to our new home to be.

A much larger dairy plant operation that we left behind, the plant and residents connected through the office. The pig sty, chicken coop and laundry room and outdoor house accessible from the enclosed yard. In one corner of the yard there was a large wooden ice shed for storage of ice that was harvested in the wintertime and buried under lots of sawdust. The town that we arrived in was in a rural area with the name Wiesenstadt in German and Wilichovo in Polish.

The plant was formerly owned by a farmer's coop, now it belonged to the German government, Father was just a manager. This part of Poland was before the 1st world war under German control and that fact was evident in later places. The only industry was the plant, distillery and agriculture, population of about 3,000. People on our arrival, 80% Polish and the rest Volksdeutche, meaning German minority for Eastern Europe, and also about 8% Reichdeutche Germans from Germany proper. The Reichdeutche were there to govern us all and considered themselves few ranks above us mere volksdeutche, yea that's life.

Major religions were Protestants and Catholics what was the fate of my family. The only medical facility were 6 Polish nuns who administrated first aid only, the nearest doctor and hospital was 20 miles away by train or horse drawn wagon. The nuns were rewarded by mother with her bounty from garden and pantry; she annoyed lots of her fellow Germans with her demonstration of good will toward the

21

nuns, our attending of Sunday mass was another annoyance of the Germans and Polish parishioners who did not appreciate our presence in the Polish church. I thought we were just good Catholics. "Damned if you do, Damned if you don't".

Father went on an improvement binge and proceeded to improve the plant extensity. Installed electrical generators and batteries for lightning the plant and residence which were lit by kerosene and carbide lamps before. New Machines were arriving at a fast pace, from refrigeration, milk storage, measuring devices, packing machines, cream storage tank with agitator; the existing machines were at least 30 yrs old. The remodeling process rewarded us with the largest bath tub in the world (remember the mind of an 8 yr old). The tub was about 10 feet long and 5 feet in the beam about 30 inches deep filled to the brim with hot water. What we had plenty of, standing in an empty room of the plant with concrete floor and drain splashing and belly flopping, what a weekly delight. The tub was a necessity with the our chores of feeding the animals, pigs, dogs, chicken, and countless pigeons not to mention rats, the rats were obliterated in short time by the improvements by father and with the help of the dogs.

The twice weekly chore of sweeping the yard and the street surrounding the plant and house, what was a must according to town, ordinance and mother's need for the natural fertilizer for her large garden. A small circus had arrived in town with few tropical animals. There were 3 monkeys on display sitting on straw bales tattered to chains. Surrounded by lots of admiring kids, some of them were feeding them small tidbits wrapped in paper, like a wise guy I wrapped a pebble and offered it to one of them, he rewarded me by grabbing my hand and sinking his teeth into my thumb, what necetate a trip to the nuns and be sent home to bed with the laughter of my buddies still ringing in my ears. I was made a monkey by a monkey.

Father also remodeled the stables and got rid of the pigs and the ice shed, chicken and pigeons stayed on in large numbers, they were good eating and handy for barter. We still slaughtered pigs, that is where the laundry room came handy with the large kettle and plenty of space to work in. mother was a very good cook and adding new recipes to extensive knowledge of Polish, Ukrainian, Germans, Jewish and Austrian Hungarian cooking and displayed on many occasions. In the very large garden attached to this property, fenced in and lined on the three sides with all kinds of fruit bushes.

The Austrian Hungarian kitchen she learned in Vienna during her time as a refugee in the First WW. She stayed with her Italian uncle, a very mysterious person, not much know by me or my siblings. Father was in the Austrian Army at that time, raising hell being promoted and busted on a regular routine. He detested people who ordered him and told him what to do. While in basic training he got himself in a very funny situation, the sergeant in charge had the recruits train in the dark with fixed bayonets. He experienced a recruit maneuver coming from the back with the bayonet very gingerly across his hand raising his hand just to be cut and bleeding threw his rifle on the stone cobble street and broke his bayonet. The sergeant after a lot of screaming and shouting provided father with a new bayonet. The problem for the authorities and his superior started with father's rebellious behavior to the point of not saluting officers and telling them to kiss his ass. That bayonet was always worn by the soldiers and its number was used as a form of ID for them, with his new bayonet he could not be traced.

When mother told me the story of her Italian uncle and that he wanted to send her to higher learning, since her ambition was to become a school teacher. Then she would have only 2 kids, that news was not received with too much joy on my part. Since being #10 I would not be writing these words. Her family nixed the idea of her uncle because of their need of her hands on the farm.

In the plant and office there were 6 Polish employees, 2 living with us. When the installation of the mechanical cooling system came later, there were benefits. The greatest was the ease of making icecream which my mother gladly indulged and all of us appreciated. The last year of over using harvested ice, I experienced and learned later new things. Harvesting the ice was quite an affair. We would hire about half a dozen teams with flat bed wagons to haul the ice from a small lake to the storage pit what had replaced the sheet in the yard, the pit was located across the plant in an open space. A group of men were busy cutting the Ice of about 10 inches to 12 inch thickness into long slabs and pulled them with metal hooks attached to wooden poles on to the ice and to the edge of the lake and then they pulled them on a makeshift ramp onto the wagons, no more than 2 high and then they proceeded to the open pit what had a bed of sawdust, layer on top of layer what became a solid block of ice, almost big enough to sink the "Titanic". Everything was covered with more sawdust and straw thatch became a make shift roof.

In summertime there were many times that we were approached for ice for sick people what we gladly obliged. Not to mention my friends who begged for slivers of ice what was a very rare and great joy to receive and to be enjoyed tremendously.

With the improvement in the plant Father raised the quality of the butter from plain county butter to first class market butter quite an achievement. Life was quite normal no ration cards, bakers, grocery store, Polish owners even Polish currency. All this was to change in less than a year we kids had mostly Polish playmates and the family associated more with Poles than Germans. The grownups associated with the Poles and remained that way all the way thru the war. Those contacts came to latter good in years of turmoil yet to come.

At this time Father engaged a private tutor to teach us 3 youngest German that we had lost to a large degree in the Polinization process of us. The Germans that we were taught was High German with no dialect inflections that is what I speak to this day. Another first for me was to see people walking in sandals with wooden soles and leather tops in winter and summer. Lots of the newcomer Germans adopted them too, mainly for the children. We in our family did not participate in this practice. In winter times the wooden soles were great to slide on the hard packed snow or ice.

The experience of may bugs in early spring was a total new happening which lasted about 14 days they came in very large swarms especially at dusk. They would get into your hair, no stinging or biting, just very distributing and creepy.

A new taste sensation molasses made from sugar beets total unknown to us and took time to get used to it. The other was a soup specialty of this region made from whey juices. Mother naturally had to try it and surprised us one evening for supper that adventure of hers was totally rejected by everyone including the live in Polish workers and was never repeated again.

The landscape had lots of windmills mostly for grinding and still operating very interesting structure quite massive riding on one center point and slightly above a supportive outer ring just shy of the bottom of the mill just flooding, just there to prevent any tipping over. The center point could be lifted to make up for wear. The winks were made of a cross pattern with wooden slots as canvas. On the other side of the winks was a large heavy timber sticking out from the structure for turning the mill into the wind, it required a team of horses and sometimes a dozen men to get it done. To stop the turning of the blades just turn it in the opposite direction. There were no brakes on them Babies.

In winter times this area had quite a lot of snowfall. Sled riding was practiced a lot on the hills or behind a horse pulling a tango line of sleds in a snake like fashion on the fields and on the roads, of course they put the girls on the end of the line just to hear them squeal and see them being whipped around in a crazy way and to be spilled of the sled with shrills screams and bruises to their egos and bodies.

With more arrival of the Reichsdutch things began to change dramatically, German currency was introduced with ration cards to follow, my father joined the Nazi party and in his enthusiasm, hung a large flag with the Swastika flanked by two oak leaf wreaths and all this topped by a spread winged eagle. The wreaths and eagle were made from paper mache coated in shiny silver. My mother who was very religious became extremely agitated and was spitting fire and flame literally, what at a later date consumed all of fathers demonstrating faith to the Nazis, all of this happened in the late 1940s.

We played a lot of games, some quite natural expressions of life around us. Playing one time with some local kids, we played a barnyard game of roosters and hens, me being a rooster. I tried to enter one of the hens just to fail as hard as I may try. On the next visit to her house for games of cards, dominos, and checkers I was made fun of and laughed at including by her parents over the failure of my performance as a rooster. In short time everything was forgotten no reprimands or reminders. Punishment was to come years later with vengeance.

With the arrival of a German teacher from the Reich school opened for us kids for grades 1 through 4 in a two room arrangement. The teacher was a workout nut who dated my oldest sister Annie, which on one occasion did not stop him for trashing my behind with a flexible metal ruler and giving me extra for not crying out.

Chapter 4
Germany Invades Russia - 1941

With the outbreak of the war against Russia, a lot of changes happened on a fast pace, father was recruited to work in the reoccupied area of our own former home for the agricultural department. He also worked for the Gastope as a translator, a fact that I didn't find out till 1990. The male teacher was drafted into the army and replaced by a female teacher barely 5 foot tall, short cropped hair with the appropriate name of "Halbeisen", English meaning "Half Iron". She handled bullies and meek sheep with her iron fist without any difficulty.

At that time a family of volksdeutche arrived across the street from our garden, their house was surrounded by a chain link fence. Brother Joe and I were standing behind a wood picket fence on fresh tilled soil, looking at 2 boys our ages behind the chain link fence staring at us. After some time with no words spoken we began to peel each other with flying objects, ours were lumps of soft soil, theirs were rocks from the driveway. Basically it was no contest and I still have a scar on my head proving the foolishment of youth. Attending the same school, we became the best of friends.

We also befriended the kids of the local game warden who was very scary to us kids and known to be mean. There were 12 kids in that family. One of the kids had the chore to go into the fields to collect ant eggs, for feed of pheasant and quail chicks, which were raised by the warden from eggs, found in the fields and turned in to him by farmers. The eggs were sat on by chickens for their hatching. For the first 2-3 weeks of growth they were fed some small kernels and also ant eggs that we had helped our friend to harvest in the forest, their nests were up to ten feet in diameter and3 feet high on the peak, totally built of pine needles by large and very aggressive Ants. We helped him on one of the chores only one time. Ant bites are no fun!

Attending the German schools we drifted away from our Polish playmates, the Polish kids started attending school that was taught by Volksdeutche teachers. One of them a very tall thin as rail man with a sour disposition who also was the father of our new friends. They moved away on a nearby farm and the family consisted of 13 kids of all ages.

On a summer school vacation, Helen and I went to visit a family friend in the provincial capital of Posen. The lady had lost her only son to the war and was a divorcee. On the second day of our stay the town was attacked by British bombers, and that sent us into the basement for shelter among screaming and crying young children, ground shaking, bombs exploding, sure scared the jibbys from us. The following morning Helen and I went to investigate just to find buildings destroyed and some shrapnel on the street, that we assumed to come from a bomb, it could also be from shells fired by a flag.

We gladly returned home to our rural surroundings just to witness a day light attack by British Bombers on an industrial area farther down the road, quite a sight shining Bombers in tide formation with dark shadows of fighters above them, in the ensuing fight about half a dozen bombers got shot down with surviving pilots taken prisoners by civilian and police, no military were in the area, the fighting high in the sky and the drum of bombers created atmosphere of a carnival happening.

Brother Joe went with some of his peers on an exploring mission to return with aluminum chare and fifty caliber ammo to show off. The sight of the amo got my sister Annie into a tirade about the nasty British and their use of such as brutal weapons against civilians, who knows it could have been Ammo from the German fighters, that's the fortune of war.

At that dramatic time changes happened in our small town. With the continued migration of Germans into the town, the Nazis removed the Polish priest and plundered the church and closed it down for the duration of the war. The nuns were also removed and replaced by a Reichsdeutche nurse of unbelievable proportion, what was hard to believe with ration cards in force, she was an ardent Nazi! The same time the village idiot disappeared from the scene, He was my sister Hedy's favorite person and she protected him against teasing and harassment with the passion of a lioness, he rewarded her with loyalty and unwilding adoration.

After his disappearance there was a definite void in her young life. She was just 16.

With the German advance into Russia and our village being liberated, my parents sent the nanny and sister Hedi, who was 16, on a scouting mission to see if we could return home. What was mothers' obsession, the danger that the two were exposed to is hard to imagine. They were almost on the German army's heels. Their negative report stopped mother's desire to return for a while and to be tired again later on in time to come.

My families' flirtation with danger of deadly consequences if discovered was a way of life with no thought of avoidance just to go forward because it was the right thing to do in our mind. My family from Rosa up had no German friends, just Poles and the same mother, not a much approved association by the German authorities. I guess the rural surroundings and distance from more frenetic Nazis was a deterrent not to prosecute us, not to forget fathers party membership and the fact he worked for the Gestapo on a part time basis. What the local authorities did not know that it was a part time only.

After Father's leaving to his new assignment he took the nanny with him, we were presented by the government with a new manager, who was of German and Polish parents, a single man who also was living in the house a very pleasant person who everybody loved to be around. Him and sister Annie became a item and got married in February 1942, what a wedding a true two day affair with family and guests in high numbers with lots of food, band, dancing, and plenty of inhibiting drinks. You mean there was a war going on where?

Something unusual happened in the winter of 1941-42. The German government appealed for warm clothes for their soldiers on the Eastern front. It was answered by the Polish and German women with quitetwo different emotions. They were making woolen shawls, warm head gear and two finger mittens and if I remember correctly one of the Polish girls won that knitting contest. Her Polish brothers did not consider her and her friends collaborating with Germans. In truth they were proud of them for having beaten the German women in that contest.

One day coming home on a dreary day I and Helen went to play some game in the boiler house. The boiler house was a detached building with access to a very large coal storage yard enclosed by a masonry wall at least ten feet tall topped with glass shards. In it was produced steam for the very large steam engine that powered all the machines by belt and pulley. The engine was enclosed by a chain link cage for safety and accessed only by the machinists. In the boiler room it was very cozy and warm and spotless. We encountered one of the Polish workers, a young man of quite long proportion, large meaning to tall and strong, we noticed his flushed face and blazing eyes, very unusual. Coming back into the house telling mother about it who also was excited, she proceeded to move us into the living room and asked us what did we see. We couldn't tell her anything, she wound up berating us of blindness and told us about ripping father's Nazi adoration off the wall and dragging it into the boiler house with instruction to that a young man to feed it into the boiler's cavernous mouth. The danger that they exposed themselves was very great and at the same time a trust built to last to the end of the war.

The aftermath of the elaborate wedding was that The nurse denounced us to the police because of the presence of Poles of the wedding. Who came and searched the house taking some of the wedding presents with them. Mother sent a telegram to father back at his job that in return sent a telegram to the local police who amazingly brought everything back and apologized to mother. I guess that the telegram from the gestope office had nothing to do with it.

During the spring of that year there was a great metal drive what was ordered by the local authorities with the result that my brother Joe was declared a winner by virtue of him having collected more reliable material than anyone else. The prize was a trip to Berlin for a parade and appearance of Hitler. They gave that award to a more ardant Nazi to the disappointment of my Brother who was quite upset about it.

Chapter 5
Life in Niesse, Poland

That year we three young ones were sent to my aunts home in the reich to attend better schools. She was my father's sister married to a local man by the name of Seibel. They lived in Selezia in the town of Neisse on the river Neisse. The town was surrounded by Earthworks erected by King "Frederick the Great" in the 18th century. The Earthworks were a haven to play and explore in. My education took a turn to the worst from straight "A's" to barely passing.

The Seibels owned a beautiful apartment building across the street from the River, only a promenade between them. They bought the building with good money and paid it off with inflated currency worth pennies. The four story building had ten foot ceilings, oversize doors and windows. For the first time I lived with running water, flushing toilets, electricity in the walls, not running on the outside of the walls, stove and oven with gas and heating with coal fired tile oven, some quite beautiful. Modern conveniences are very easy to get used to. The running water was supplied by lead pipes and consumed daily. Lead poisoning. Ha, not me! Ah what did you say? I can't remember.

My life was quite nice on the home front and very disturbing on the schooling side. I became withdrawn with tendencies to day dream looking out the window which earned me a few times a slap on my face. I started Sunday school and began instruction for my first confession in preparation for 1st communion. To my sorrow and torture I discovered what a big sinner I was to have played the rooster in a harmless kids play. The torment of that knowledge and the continuous drumming in of the fact what a deadly sin I committed, so I dreaded the day of first confession. The day finally arrived and on entering confessional stall I blurted out to the priest I have "Fucked", those exact words and at the same time sweating and with a racing heart expecting to die, the horror of this day was never to be forgotten. The priest must have been aware of my tortured state of mind and without any question or reprimands he gave me a few prayers for absolution. The four letter word that I had just used was not in common use in my youth and I never heard it from any family member, I guess something that I had picked up on the street. The load lifted off me and my tormented soul was definitely exhilarating to say the least.

This mayhem caused by well meaning righteous people teaching Sunday school is deplorable and outright a form of child abuse. For the first communion I got a brand new suit, made from the English fabrics obtained by my father and received by God fearing "holier than thou" his sister. The same one who condemned my mother to Hell and didn't mind to tell us kids of that fact. In retrospect was my right of first communion, so to speak legal, I wonder going to the alter in stolen goods was accepted by the good lord.

Next I joined the Hitler youth voluntarily. Let me explain, it even surprised me. During classes we got interrupted by a band of about six senior Hitler youth in full uniform and asked of our ages. Everybody ten years and older had to stand up and give our names and addresses and on completion of this task they informed us that we had joined the Hitler youth voluntarily and reminded to attend twice weekly meetings, which was not received with much enthusiasm because it interfered with homework and especially playtime, in the Earthworks, in town and on the river.

War had little impact on us because of the rural setting no industry except a military installation on the outskirts of town who were involved in motorized infantry training sometimes the vehicle would tremble through the streets of the town. On few occasions we see we saw allied bombers in daylight heading for the industrial part of Silisia. On the way to school we would pass British prisoners of war driving horse teams with freight mostly of flour, wheat and potatoes to and from the train station. We kids were delighted to greet them with a hardy good morning in English which was returned with a warm smile and wave of hand. The prisoners looked quite well fed in a great contrast to the pitiful looking Russian prisoners. We were afraid to greet them not because of them but because of the guards.

During the summer recess in 1943 we kids visited father and the nanny in Lvov. She took us on a visit to a museum that was located on the side of a steep hill which contained battle scenes by a famous Polish king, who lifted the siege of Vienna by the Turkish sultan in the 17th century. The Poles having just arrived on the scene late in the evening and without any rest attacked the overwhelming Force of the sultan who were already bedded down for the night. This drove the Turks into flight to abandon camp leaving everything behind including the sultan's treasure.

The enjoyment of that pleasurable experience was to be short lived and ended in dreadful memories that will last me to the day of my death. On leaving the panoramic museum we proceeded to a coffee ice cream parlor on the base of that hill. Sitting on the porch of said establishment and looking across the street at the base of another steep hill with freshly distributed soil of yellow sand. The nanny announced the reason for the disturbances was the fact that Ukrainian collaborators of the Nazis had killed and buried Jewish women and children on that site. That news brought an instant reaction in me, I began to see the soil to roil and heave; lost all appetite for the ice cream and insisted to go home to the frustration of the nanny. That gruesome discovery was to haunt me all of my life till I found some peace in the year 2004.

I shall jump ahead and tell what happened in the year 2004. My current wife Patricia Maloney, a native born in Washington DC, and I went on a visit to the place of my birth. Staying in the Lvov in a hotel we took a tour of the town with the specific goal to find the infamous hill with the graves of the Jewish women and children. Asking local people didn't get me anywhere. Having a German speaking guide and his college age daughter as a companion we found the panorama hill with its platform on top. This Polish museum was replaced by a television station and its towers. The museum was dismantled and shipped to Poland. Arriving at the top of the platform on top of the hill and looking around I discovered the yellow sand hill instantly. Being told by the college student that she recalled having heard a professor talking about the massacre on the base of the hill. The Russians had built a textile factory to try to obliterate the graveside and so any association of the Ukrainian brother in that heinous crime. The next day me and my wife went to the hill with a beautiful bunch of flowers and I climbed halfway up and planted the flowers on said hill saying a prayer in memory of this not forgotten people. With some soil and wild flowers that I picked on the hill for me to bring to the USA and forwarding it to a synagogue for their remembrance and prayers for the holy people. My belief in doing this is my reward.

My father took sister Helen and I on a fact-finding tour through Ukrainian villages including on that trip was a beautiful red headed secretary of my father, his lover. Brother Joe who was absent was in a hospital for surgery to correct a birth defect. We

all engaged in good food and generous hospitality
by the Ukrainian farmers and slept 2 nights in hay
lofts with blankets as bedding; this was all 4 of us.

On a trip downtown usually for ice cream the
nanny, my sister Helen and me witnessed the only
casualty of the war, riding on the street car we
witnessed a shoot out between German military
police and some Polish partisans involved in a
robbery of a supply truck and the only death was an
innocent street car track switch man, just a
bystander. We lost our appetite for ice cream and
went home. There next to the ice cream place was a
Woolworths store and the nanny never forgot to
point it out. That was the first time I was aware of
the USA existence.

Meanwhile things were happening on the home
front, in rapid pace, my brother in law was drafted
into the army and later captured by the Americans
and taken to the USA. On his departure my sister
Anni became the manager of the plant at a very
young age, she was just 23, quite an achievement
and definitely earned. She kept that position until
the arrival of the Russians in January 1945.

On one occasion in the spring of 1944 we had a big
assembly of the whole school on the Earthworks
surrounding the town. We were given speeches and
propaganda where the principal in full Nazi
Uniform who broke down and cried in front of us
kids, complaining about what was to come dreading
the day of reckoning and arrival of the Russians.

What dumbfounded us kids was the peace and lack of any upheaval in the area plus we were winning, right! The odd thinking of us kids was that Hitler was the savior and he was being betrayed by his associates, in the end he would come out on top and win all for us. In my opinion one of the biggest crimes of the Nazis was the brainwashing of the German youth.

The disillusion of the grownups of the Nazis became manifested in small deeds and gestures. As I found out later father was buying and hoarding gold American coins that he found on the black market. He also kept his prewar Polish passport that he obtained on his visit to his sister which identified him as a Polish citizen. These two facts were to save his life in less than a year.

While living and going to school at my aunt's place, me and her went on a visit of a distant family member by the name Apelman, this was my grandmother's name on my father's side. The visit was social and for economical reasons; To obtain extra eggs, smoked meat products, and water was available to fill her pantry. Talking about the pantry my aunt was quite a good cook and we got to learn few new dishes. Domestic rabbits, which we raised ourselves, were quite often on the table. There was a small garden in the yard with a stable for rabbits. My cousin and I went during the growing season to a field on the outskirts of town to fetch red clover. My aunt had obtained permission from the farmer to harvest. We would go once a week and bring 2 large sacs on the bicycles, some would be fed fresh to the 1 ½ to 2 dozen rabbits that were in the cages, the rest dried for hay. Scraps from kitchens of all kinds also would be fed to them mixed with oat kernels. Hungry we were never. The pelts from the rabbits were very desired for lining in overcoats and such.

Chapter 6
Back Home Again – Wiesenstadt

In the summer of 1944 we returned home for good. On the return we had an upsetting experience especially for my sister Rosa. The German ration cards were in the form of large sheets similar to postal stamps, perforated with a sheet per person according to age and what labor they performed. On it were stamps for different food groups and on each purchase the proper stamps was removed and kept by the retailer who in turn had to glue them to large sheets of paper like newspaper separated by food groups that were totaled on the bottom of each page, then totaled for easy counting by the proper authorities.

On one evening of this chore in the retail store for dairy products in the company of a Polish girl, she was held up, slapped and all the sheets with the glued on stamps were stolen to be used in the black market. If it was resistance members I hope it was, for distributing large amounts of dairy products from the wholesaler market for the use of their needy people. We assumed that the holdup was accomplished with an inside information because the timing was too good if you consider no telephone, no radio, just mouth to mouth communication. I hope it was for a good cause.

On the return from Neisse, Brother Joe became quite a rebel, causing disturbances with the local youths of his age, especially the Hitler youths. To the point that the police came to the house and warned mother to control him or face the consequences of him disrupting the weekly Hitler youth meetings and marching. That harassing earned him a couple of slaps in the face from the Hitler youth leader, a boy about twice the size of my brother. That bully was walking back to his marching troupes when halfway down the field my brother caught up with him and swiftly spun him around landing his fist into the bully's face. Brother immediately high tailed out of there leaving the bully bleeding from mouth and nose in front of all the troops of Hitler boys who began laughing that in turn brought that meeting to an abrupt end for the day. I guess my brother had a driving need for revenge since the bully was rewarded with the trip to Berlin that my brother had earned in that metal drive.

Brother entered an apprenticeship at a railroad yard repair shop to become a machinist. While Helen and me enrolled in a nearby town for junior high, a boarding school. Sister Helene had no trouble getting in- me, that was another story, Just passing was not a much desired grade in that school. Mother and I went to see the school superintendent for the county and on entering his office mother announced herself with a resounding " Gruss Gott". His reply was "hail Hitler" was the proper greeting for my mother just to shoot back not when I come in. His eyes shot open and seeing mother red faced and fire spitting eyes dropped that subject and inquired for the reason of our presence. He granted our request without any more fanfare, I guess just to get rid of that bothersome tigress in human disguise. The irony of that situation was his party membership buttons was in gold stating to the fact that he was a member of the party before 1932.

That same year the Nazis recognized the local mothers by the number of kids they had and awarded them with medals. Mother received one in front of an assembly group of people and officials in "gold" with a swastika in the center. This medal was very much appreciated and a source of pride for her. The school was half the distance between the county seat and our town, about 15 miles distance, public transportation consisted of narrow rail train, and what was pulled by a very cute steam engine and a delight to ride on. Sometimes we would ride to other places in an open coach with retractable roof, upholstered seat riding down the highway lined with horse chestnuts and Linder trees, what an experience. The occasional meeting of a motorized vehicle caused some antics and scary moments mostly solved by the driver pulling to the side and covering the horses faces to let the stinkbugs pass.

All through the war there were usually 2 maids employed, one Polish girl to keep her from forced labor in the "Reich" and a Volksdeutche from the black sea area of Russia. From her talking she and her family were die hard Russians and resented the forced resettlement tremendously. She was a beautiful girl about 19 years of age, Brother Joe and I absolutely adored her. She was a real tomboy and beat us on any game that we played, to mother's disgust she would drop anything she was doing just to amuse herself and anger us by being better at anything we had done.

The loyalty that the black sea Germans had for Russia was rewarded by Stalin to have them forcefully resedelt to Kazikstan a place to play an important role in my family's lives in the near future. One of our neighbors next to the plant was a big park with a chateau in the center surrounded by brick and wooden fences six foot high with locked gates. The entry was forbidden for us mere peasants.

Arriving and beginning classes were good to learn English, algebra, and Latin, a very sore subject with me. On weekends we would go home on the cute train to recoup our strength. The classes in this school were less rigid, plus no Hitler youth meetings, hard to believe since the principal was an ardent Nazi, in late December with the Russian approach from the East everybody was sent home and most local Germans were packing to retread and flee to the Reich including sister Rosa and

brother Joe. One 18, and the other 16. They made it
barely to Bavaria and stayed there till after the war.

Before they left, mother prepared her form of iron
ration for their trip. It was peanut colored roe with
some salt and caraway seeds in a small milk can of
about 1 ½ gallons a second can would contain
cooked sausage stored in pork lard for keeping. this
survival kit was used by mother all the time if any
of us departed for unknown destinations. It
definitely helped us to survive, for the rue all you
needed was hot water and instant nourishing soup.
Or you could eat it by chewing part of it and
washing it down with water. Quite an energy giver
just like the story says, Mother Knows Best.

Chapter 7
The Russian Occupation - 1944

Before sister and brother left, father had arrived
home, being a deserter from the volkstorm on New
Year's Eve 1944. He stayed with us for the next 10
days to witness the Russian entry and our moving
from the plant to a one room with a cooking stove
in a Polish friend's house, seven people in one
room. Father was arrested by the Russian town
commander on accusation of being a Nazi. With
knowledge of the Russian language, his prewar
Polish passport, and being little of a con man he
was released, hit the streets running, never turned
around or said goodbye just to avoid being
rearrested on evidence brought by some of his
accusers, showing him in the Nazi party uniform. to

the commander who sent an arresting party to apprehend him. Of course father was not to be found anywhere.

The conditions were chaotic to say the least, no civil communications existed. It was not in the Russian commanders' best interest to find my father. One reason for this easy gateway was that there were a lot of elderly men roaming like lost souls through the country side and one more didn't arouse any suspicion. We would find out by letter in about 4-5 months that he was alive and prospering.

We lost almost all of our personal property to plunder and it was not resented by mother, just the ways of the war. What my mother did resent was the fact that the alter covers she had made by hand for the plundered Polish church were not returned by the wife of one of the workers in the plant whom she had entrusted for safe keeping. In the end that was better than if she had it returned. Faith has funny ways of playing itself out. Mother somehow retained her golden Nazi medal and finally abandoned it in an outhouse. She really hated to part from it.

Sister Hedy, 19yrs, and the Nanny had to report daily for some cleaning duties from streets to churches, being supervised by Young Polish men who didn't mind to tease and make fun of therm. After the Russian arrival, my sister Hedy had a confrontation with a young, Russian NCO, to the point that he pulled his handgun and cocked it, and she stupidly kept calling him dumb and stupid. Go figure that one out—she got away with it. She's still alive, and living in Baden, Prince George County, MD.

At one point in the first few weeks of the Russian occupation, I was sent by the Polish family to deliver a message to the bookkeeper in the plant to report to the Russian commander in charge of the town. On the way to the plant I ran into a Polish boy my age who I knew from having played with him. He proceeded to take his belt off and tried to hit me. I disarmed him so to speak and hit him instead then gave him his belt back and threatened to report him to the commander of the town. He had enough of me and didn't bother me anymore. I proceeded to the plant and delivered the message. You wonder why the boy wanted to show me his superiority, what really was not there because of the Russians presents what overshadowed everything.

The Russian commander power was life and death. On one occasion after 3 days of open city he declared an end to plundering and occasional rape of the Polish women by the Russian troops. A drunk Russian private went on a rampage and was reported to the commander who had him shoot behind a barn and gave the Poles instruction to bury him right on the spot, I personally saw the grave no marker of any kind. What a pitiful waste of a human being.

Chapter 8
Another Resettling – Kazakstan?

With the establishment of civil government in town, normality and new currency arrived. At the same time the Russians started to register some of their citizens in that area, some forced labor, and most that were refugees from the communist and collaborates with the Nazis to return them home, what very few got to see, unless you consider Siberia home. Mother registered for that resettling in her belief that we would be shipped to our home village. That voluntary registration saved us later mistreatment and hard labor for years to come.

Shortly after our departure, the Poles put all Germans in their jurisdiction into work camps and where very stressful conditions existed and thousands perished. Grandma was one of the people. They were especially mean against the former citizens of Poland who were accused of treason and treated with extreme cruelty. By mother's foolish beliefs we were to be going home would solve all of the problems and in a very weird way it did. Hurray for women's intuition.

We consisted of grandma, mother, nanny, Hedy, Helene and me. We took off with a couple hundred other hopeful people on the 16th of march towards Russia in boxcars and with belongings that you could carry, on a journey of unforgettable moments in time, some happy, others extremely sad. You had no time to dwell on it just always forging forward and hoping for a brighter day and it actually did come, what a ride in destiny. Never dreaming that in over year we would be back in west Germany safe and sound. Going through Lodz, a central Polish industrial town on our stop over to Russia, mother contacted her younger sister who was married to a Polish shoemaker by the name of Smyk, who was in the Polish army. Mother talked her sister into taking grandma off the train which is what she did. Helene and I went to see grandpa at the basement apartment where they lived and we found grandpa sitting in a chair. He was beat up and bleeding due to the handiwork of some Polish thugs. He died in a few days, yea that's war.

We returned to the train station to another tragedy. The Russian had shot a switchman for being drunk and causing a small collision of trains. In this kind of situation the Russians were very strict and ruthless and would not tolerate infraction regardless of who you were or what. We continue our way to the promised land and arriving in Lublin and staying there for a few days.

The nanny somehow convinced mother to try to stay in Poland because the Russians were retreating and the Germans would be back and rescue us. Then we could find father again, it was absolutely a crazy idea and not to mention very dangerous. A Polish Mob had in the previous months massacred a trainload of German nurses on the way to Russia just for them being Germans, that's war. So my sister Hedy and our Russian friend on that train came up with a story that they had seen my father on a prisoner of war train going to Russia and he waved to them and was very sickly looking. That persuaded our mother to continue the trip to Russia. Thank God.

Then we continued on to the Russia border on this stretch of the railroad ride through Poland, between the town of Lublin and all the way to the Russian border. The banks of the railroad spurs were covered with German money in the millions and millions, nothing more than trash, so we thought. We arrived in Brest on the border a Russian town, our family was taken off the train and ordered into a processing/prisoner of war camp where I seen for the first time German prisoners of war.

After a week stay in the camp we were issued papers to precede to Kasakstan, remember the "black sea Germans". Sent back to the train with all the Russian refugees we were issued bread and canned Argentinian beef, quite good tasting to last us for 14 days. On returning to the condemned people we were told by them there was no place for us except in an empty box car that was not going where they were "Siberia". True gossip in the camp we know the destination of that ride to hell.

A family that we know from Wiesenstadt joined us in our car, mother, 2 children, and grandparents who were from the general area that we were to pass through. Shortly before midnight we were disconnected and attached to another train and started to roll into an uncertain future. There were no guards or a designated party to oversee anything, just false promises and people believing in unfaltering word of the government. I guess the government was busy fighting a war against the Nazis, so the few people consisting mostly of women, children, and broken down elderly were not much of importance.

As we rolled in the general direction of our former home and passing through the badly destroyed town of Kovel, few miles out of that town, while we were stopped on a bypass spur to let trains going in the other direction through, all of us disembarked and walked the few miles back to the train station in Kovel to camp out there and to obtain some money by selling some sugar that we owned on a farmers market. That sugar about 5 pounds in our luggage was worth its weight in gold and definitely kept us alive, the carryon luggage consisted of one good size wicker basket with two stout handles on each end and few sacks over the shoulder. Nothing beats traveling in style.

With the money we obtained tickets to our friend's hometown where we arrived in a day or so, again the train was nothing more than box cars with wooden planks for seats, hey a ride is a ride. Arriving at our goal the friends preceded to their families in outlying villages, we camped out with a Polish family in town, given refuge by their daughter who worked on the train station. I remember sleeping under the table in the kitchen on a blanket on the floor with my younger sister.

After a few days we got our marching orders so to speak. Local police started to make inquiries about all the extra people, so we decided the prudent thing to do was to move on, my mother rewarded the Polish girls with a pair of new medium high heel shoes of the same size and design except one brown and one black. I know you ask how that was possible. Before the Russian liberation, my aunt who was married to the Polish shoemaker operated a shoe store in Lodz, she had sent a large wooden crate with shoes to our house for safe keeping what was ultimately plundered by the Poles and that one pair saved by our nanny. The young lady was overwhelmed by the gift and did not hesitate to announce she would make them look alike with no trouble.

We proceeded to the train station and approached the Russian trainmaster for free tickets to Lvov. He denied us of this, then on announcing to camp in his station and showing him papers for Kasikstan, he was persuaded to issue us free tickets. This traveling papers to Kasikstan, which I have a copy of the one issued to my sister Hedy, had only information of our destination , no telephone number or address of issuing authority, yea they did have the ever present big stamp of totalitarian bureaucracy.

On our arrival in Lvov we proceeded to the home of
our prewar salesman Urban who was in the army at
that time and were given refuge by his wife and 17
year old son. They lived on the outskirts of town in
a good size house with a garden. In a few days the
nanny left to go home about 25 miles away where
she stayed for the next 7 months.

The same day late in the evening Russian soldiers
arrived surrounding the house searching and
arresting us. Then dragging us through the streets,
from one station to another just to question us and
wanting to know how did we get here. They never
abused or searched us, finally locking us up in a
make shift jail for some political and dissonant
prisons in an apartment house. We were assigned to
an empty room to sleep on bare floors, no food or
drink, luckily fellow prisoners who had food
brought by their families shared some with us.

Our presence caused confusion for the local police,
they did not know what to do with this group of
Germans who had arrived with no papers of any
identification and crossing borders really a very
ticklish situation. To this day I can't fathom the
indecisiveness of the Russians, why they didn't
shoot us and get rid of that problem, you have to
know there was a war going on and Russian soldiers
were killed by the thousands. I guess the distance
from the war theatre and their consistent obsession
to withhold such information from their public.

Chapter 9
Back to My Home Village

After a week of detention we were brought into the office of a commissioner and told by him thanks to the Russian people we were to be released and had to leave the town in 24 hours. My mother and my 2 sisters obliged that order and guess who they left behind me to stay with a Polish official railroad employee who was from our village and still with families there.

Staying with this family was also a Russian young army recruit a pitiful sight no more than 18-19 yrs old in a sloppy uniform and a blanket and knapsack as his whole possession, he arrived every evening just to cook some gruel a type of Russian iron ration. A rather shy person totally intimidated by his Polish hosts. After a few days of stay a man arrived with a horse drawn wagon announcing that he was sent to pick me up by my mother to take me to her.

I was delivered to the train employee's family's house to assist them in the farm operation. That family consisted of grandma, daughter in law, and two young boys, one 6 years and the other 9 months. The father was in the army. I became the caretaker for 2 cows and one horse, the chore required me to fetch water from a neighbors well carrying the 2 buckets suspended on a yoke over my shoulder, it took about 3 trips and 3 times a day.

After morning feeding and watering of the animals I would take the cows to graze, they were tied around their horns to a 15 foot rope between them and me in the middle, describing the cows as frisky was an understatement of global proportion. At one of my forays into the fields for their grazing they escaped my grip of the rope and it took over 2 hours of hard chasing to apprehend them again, not because of my persistence, but of their total exhaustion was I able to get a hold of them. That day there was not any milk to be gotten and I wound up with a stern warning not to let it happen again, I should have known better after all I was a 13 year old "damn stupid boy".

My sleeping bed consisted of a wooden bench of some proportion and quite common in this area with a wooden lid that was hinged on one side and leaned against the wall, revealing a course burlap sack stuffed with straw, if you were lucky it would be straw from oats which was soft and pliable. My rolled up jacket as a pillow and course blanket as a cover most the time sleeping in the clothes you wore during that day without the boots naturally "manners we did have!" my biggest nightmare was the lid leaning against the wall, that fell on me one night awoke me quite rudely and taught me not to stir or turn to much while sleeping.

After a few days on the next weekend "Sunday half day". I got to visit my mother and youngest sister four houses down the street. They stayed with the former maid of my grandmother, she was a mother with infant, husband in the army with one cow and couple acres of ground. Sister Helene became the designated babysitter and mother helped out in the stable and field. Mother also did barter work for the local women with her great skill of sewing. In this barter she obtained staples for everyday living also feed for her host's cow.

Sister Hedy I didn't see till weeks later. She lived and worked with the Polish farmers' wife who had bought our farmstead and land from my parents in the prewar days. He was in the army just his wife no children, one male farm hand, very unusual. Sister was just another hand in need because they had 3 cows, 2 horses, pigs and chickens, a sign of a better farmer.

On one encounter with sister Hedy I experienced a happening never to be forgotten on the Pentecost Sunday. Arriving for high mass in a nearby village, shortly after my arrival with my youngest sister Helene I was slapped in the face on the steps of the church for wearing my best clothes I owned, that suit (remember English wool) dated back to my first communion 2 years ago, I definitely had outgrown it. Some young men in older sister's circle made fun of that and teased her unmercifully so she let her anger out on me and to this day she is still a very mean person and her kids can testify to this. And on the other hand quite generous to strangers.

We all were quite in good humor and enjoyed life as best as we could. The village had changed dramatically. We were the only Germans. All the German homestead were settled with Ukrainian newcomers to the village. The old rivalry between the Poles and Ukrainians came to the surface again especially in the villages far from town it went to the point of robbery and murder. One of the Ukrainian newcomers lost 2 sons to that old hatred. The boys were drafted in a roundup by the Russians and were being marched in columns to a mustering camp. Few miles from home, the brothers escaped and were hiding in a barn owned by Poles. One woman went to the commanding non-com in the marsh and betrayed the brothers who were dragged out from the barn and positioned in front of the halted columns where the non-com shot both men to death. Their father picked them up after 2 days he found them where they had fallen. The power of the Russian non in war time was unbelievable.

The ethnic change that was to come was the best thing the Russians did for the misguided people. My employer the wife of the farmer was vain to a degree mean, not so much to me as to her mother in law, a very nice lady. This lady told me occasionally about her experience during the German occupation in 1942. The Polish farmers of that village had to give up their property for the new arrival of German minorities' arriving from Russia. The farmers had to report to the local school to register to receive their marching orders. on entering seeing a young women's face that they recognized as a former resident of that village just to be told by that 20 yr old runny nosed kid that only German will be spoken here. What a shock to people already stressed out and in dire need of compassion. The only way to describe this uncaring person is to reveal her name "Maria Hupert" my second oldest sister. that experience bothered this old lady a lot because I got to hear it a few times without rancor towards me only bitterness and her disappointment.

A typical day for me began with early rise meaning barely daytime to feed and water the animals in the stable, consume my daily breakfast, a wedge of bread washed down with cold low fat milk (a very modern concept). What a modern concept. The low fat milk was achieved by a primitive process. Freshly obtained milk would be poured into special cylinder containers, that had at the bottom a small glass window and a short open funnel next to it. What was plugged up with a potato. The cylinder was lowered into the well just stuck a few inches above the water. That water was 50 degrees or less. Cream would rise to the top and next morning brought into the house to harvest the cream by removing the potato, watching the glass window for the cream to arrive which was collected and stored in the pantry for two times weekly butter making.

The side benefit was buttermilk for our consumption. This milk obtained this way was for daily consumption and surplus to make cottage cheese. What was sold together with the butter on farmer's market day still practiced and permitted by the Russians. The trip to town of 3 miles distance was always undertaken by the young women, butter and cottage cheese was wrapped in horseradish leaves that are quite large and in wintertime in pots and pans. Customers at that market always brought their own containers. on occasion also fresh eggs sometimes she walked or when lucky was offered a ride by a friendly farmer with a wagon and a horse. That money she obtained was usually spent on things for the kids or herself and sometimes on cookies from Germany offered by returning Russian soldiers. She never bought anything for her mother in law or me.

I did help myself sometimes to the cookies that were hidden in a very large hope chest. Then out to grazing with my charges held in my closed fist, to return at noon for the same routine, water feed the cows and horses and also me. This time boiled potatoes sometimes with a drop of butter just to wash it down with water or buttermilk if available. Then back to the fields and return before nightfall while still daylight left for the chores and supper to be done.

The neighbor to the right of my employer was a Ukrainian farmer and part time shoemaker who was exempt from the army because of some ailment. He and his wife had 2 sons the older a humpback and best bare back horse rider I ever seen , riding that Indian pony looking horse like he was welded to it, no reigns nothing just to control it with a small switch to do his bidding at full speed and hooping and hollering like he was possessed.

The younger one my age was named Iwasho who was lots of times my companion in the fields, grazing over cows together. Except he had the most docile of 2 animals that would never stray from him being let go of the rope on their own. The rope he only used for driving them from pasture to home or other ways around. I definitely was very jealous of that fact.

With the new growth of animal food there was another chore to be done. Twice weekly for this harvesting, the young women of the house would go to the field with horse drawn wagons to fetch some feed for the cows to increase their milk output. She would cut the green wedge with a scythe and I would load it on the wagon lifting it to her and in return distributed it on the wagon. This green feed would be quite wet from dew and so not getting her skirt soaking wet, she would hitch it up and reveal her privates right into my face without batting an eye. That moment had me bewildered and almost scared at the same time a strange magnetic pull to see more, yeah the rights to grow up are many and definitely mysterious.

The local women didn't wear any underpants summer or winter nor did they own any. My modesty was severely tested on another occasion, encountering a widow with a cow, exchanging some pleasantries about spring or weather she was sitting down about 30 feet away and had her cow tethered to a stake in the ground. We were approached by a

Russian soldier, who was staying in the village with the local police/mayor. The two began chatting just a few words and next I know he pushed her over from sitting position onto her back and began copulating. That was finished in a jiffy , stood up and proceeded down the fields. This episode made me understand the saying of "wham bam thank you ma'am". There was no exchange of any pleasantry or momentary love, what so ever, just wanton lust of the moment. She sat up and continued talking to me like nothing had happened, sure confused the hell out of me. She gave birth to a son in early 1946,not all education comes from street gutter, some in meadows in bloom.

Experiences come in all dimension and let me tell you about one that I treasure to this day. During early summer hay cutting time I was sent to the fields to deliver a message to an elderly Polish farmer who was helping out In the harvest of the hay. He was one of about 4 men who did the cutting with a scythe to see them perform, one following the other with about 10 feet of space between them in rhythm and making small talk. A very impressive sight. And the smell of freshly cut grass was to die for. On the way back to the village this elderly man talked to me in a manner like a sage full of wisdom and kindness, something I never experienced before or after from anybody. To see this man was something not to forget. His clothes were homespun cloth trousers and a shirt from the same material almost reaching to his knees with no collar only 4 buttons on the top of the shirt. Everything was held in place by a black belt with a whetstone holder to sharpen the scythe.

My friend next door went to visit a sister of his mom's about 8 miles distance and returned with treasures of a spectacular nature chains of 30 caliber machine gun ammo and powder charged from large caliber artillery shells which were in a stick form about 16 inches in length and 2 inches in diameter. One hole of ¼ through the length of the powder.

On the following Sunday while grazing the cows behind the barn I had them tethered to a tree. We proceeded to light the powder charge with difficulty. Finally one of the sticks ignited on one end and began burning at a very intense rate and drawing the air through the small whole the length of it. That created a nose straight from hell that brought out half the village behind the barns to our chagrin. We could not extinguish the fire and had to let the oversize fire cracker do its thing. That mischief sure got a lot of people excited and angry at us. The machine gun ammo we separated the bullets from the shells and saved everything for some fun at a later date.

The bullets from machine gun belts have tracers every 6-8 bullets, on one occasion having a small bonfire in the fields we threw the tracers into the fire and retreated to safe distance. After a few minutes nothing happened and we returned to the fire and just before arriving the tracer started to go off scaring the hell out of us, me trying to run with the cows, each going a different direction. What a disaster. After a minute the tragedy subsided and some sorts of calm returned to us. Tracers don't explode. How do we know that, "not us!"

On another occasion, I witnessed 2 women returning from town and trekking home; they stopped and one woman proceeded to urinate right on the path next to us standing erect with her legs parted and holding her skirt front away from her body. It sounds gross but really is not. They never wore panties and probably didn't own any.

Any packages being brought home from the market were carried in large blanket- like wraps which was slung over one shoulder and under one arm, then tied together in front, giving them a hands free situation. Landscape in that area was completely treeless and bushes only in swampy areas, everything was quite flat with no place to hide. They had done their best with what they had; restrictive modesty or false pretense had no room in their lives.

The Galizian Germans and Jews were not as liberated as the Polish and Ukrainian peasants, what a shame. In June 1945 the Russians began an ethnic cleansing program, the Poles had to register for resettlement to former parts of Germany annexed to Poland after the capture of this territory from the Germans and also as composition for territories taken by the Russians from Poland.

They were shipped to bigger and much more modern farms planted and managed by their former German owners who were to stay on for a duration of harvesting and to teach the newcomers the new knowledge of modern farming, some learned and became successful farmers, others declined all the new technology and lost everything after the departure of the German owners, that departure was just around the bend.

On leaving their homestead there was a lot of crying and hand wringing understandable for what these people had undergone in the last few year. In a very short time of 2 weeks, the first trains of loaded box cars, left for Poland and to be followed by some trains in succession. My oldest sister left with her employer on this first train. Shortly before her departure we received a letter from our lost father who sent it to his Ukrainian friend in the village who was the some family of the Ukrainian wedding I witnessed before the war. He asked him for assistance to help him in locating us.

Here we were, father had saved his friends lives and some Jews while working for the Gastopo during the German occupation. Having found out that the Germans were to search his friend's farmstead he took on himself to lead the riding party of about four army privates commandeered for that foray arriving and speaking to his friend in private and in Ukrainian searched the location of the hiding place and declared it empty sending the soldiers on a wild goose chase thus saving his friend and the Jews he was hiding. Father claimed that the hiding place was next to a pig pen in piles of straw, what an irony for the Jews saved by pigs.

He gave the letter to my mom and we found out that he was living in the former home town of his sister in Neisse which was now in Poland. He opened a bakery and had found our oldest sister with her son, she had taken refuge with her in-laws just before the Russian entry. So sister Hedy had a destination when she left without even saying goodbye. My employer left at the same time and rewarded me with some home spun handmade yards of fabric dull and grey in color, mother at a later date sewed me some workpants from it, extremely durable material. She also gave me about half acre of standing wheat in the field.

The new arrivals were Ukrainians of the other side of the border who were sent east, luckily for me the new owner honored the gift of the growing wheat to me. You never know where kindness would show up, always in the most unusual places and in my experiences it was shown by people of every rank in life.

After the departure of my employer I began working for the local policeman/mayor who was illiterate and good natured, not too bright. Before war, he earned his living as a day worker and found him quite lazy. He and his wife had 2 kids, girls, one my age and the other an infant. That poor infant suffered horrible colic, probably gotten from mother's milk.

On one occasion they brought in a witch, my eyes sure got bigger and bigger. First they put a broom made from birch twigs leaning against the wall by the entrance to the room. Then the witch got some glowing coals from the cooking stove and proceeded to mumble and gyrate around the child's cradle while spitting on the floor. What a sight never to be forgotten. Did it help, Hell no, I understand that child survived to become a grown up.

There were 2 cows and 2 horses in the stable and they lived on a farm previously owned by Germans. My chore was the same as before, the food was definitely better, the meat about twice a month, plenty of fruit from the orchard. This farmstead was across from where my mother stayed and I visited her almost daily, most of the time with fresh fruits which she, sister, and maid didn't mind at all.

I liked my new employment a lot. It was my place of work and to eat. I slept in my friend's house in the hayloft. My boss was not much of a farmer and if it was not for his father in law, not much would have been done on the fields of this farm; with 2 horses in the stable both being obtained from the booty. The Russians were dragging them from conquered territory in Europe to Russia. Big herds of horses were driven through the country side and ones arriving in Russian territory were given away just for asking most of these animals died because of lack of proper care and feed, what a waste. One of the horses was a small mare of quite nice nature. I tried to learn how to ride local style bareback and no reigns, just a short rope to control the animal. After a few minutes a pitiful attempt to control this horse, she had enough of me and run under low hanging limbs of an apple tree and swept me off her back with gusto. The last thing I saw while on the ground was her rear end disappearing back into the stable. I had to endure the laughter from my friends.

On one occasion as the new crops were harvested we ran out of flour for bread baking. The elder daughter and I had to trash some wheat with a flail what took us one afternoon and next day we proceeded to a relative's house in the nearby village to an antique building with a hand driven grindstone for grinding the kernels for flour needed to bake some bread. That grinding was quite strenuous and hard to accomplish.

While we were at our chore I observed glowing cinder flowing from the chimney which protruded about 16 inches above the attic floor. The smoke dissipated through an opening in the gable ends. This old house was built in typical fashion, rectangle with entrance to a central hall going the full depth of the house at least than 12-16 feet wide. No ceiling, just exposed rafters, the roof straw thatch on one side and contained 2 rooms and the other side stables, both sides had attic space for storage and also extra sleeping area. The two rooms were just divided by a wall and the oven was for bread baking and also heating the house in winter time. The entrance to the oven was from the central hall, what was also a place to prepare our daily chores needed on the farm. Wood chopping or prepare feed for the livestock and cooking on brick hearth in front of the oven. Cooking was done on an open fire with pots and pans sitting on a triangle device.

The majority of the Ukrainian and Polish peasants ate mostly boiled food in one form or another. In my 7 months there I have not eaten anything fried or roasted or any baked pastry of any kind, except what I have snitched from the hope chest of my former boss, and that was the booty of Russian soldiers brought back from Germany.

The walls of the house were wooden frame and covered with clay mixed with straw of about 12 inch thickness. The white wash was the only color that I have ever seen. In the winter this house would be wrapped in one and a half inch thickness of straw held to the wall with the help of wooden poles, not a very pleasant sight and then again not freezing.

On a big thrash day performed by a primitive thrashing machine driven by a turntable pulled by a team of horses, I was busy carrying thrashed wheat to the attic for further drying and slipped on the very steep steps and fell back to catch myself and never dropped the sack of wheat, no more than 50 pounds, developing a hernia needing a makeshift belt that my mother made to hold my gut in. With the belt I felt as good as new and ready for all kinds of mischief.

Late in the waning days of fall 1945 I had an awakening of my sexuality. While grazing with my friends Iwasho and "Kukoraciak" meaning Banty Rooster, the three of us encountered 3 girls from a nearby village also grazing their cows and proceeded to press them for a sexual encounter which they gladly would oblige with the stipulation not to have Kukoraciak present. He was about 2 years younger than us. On our pushing and shoving he refused to leave and so we failed in our attempt to become men, at least in our eyes.

With bad weather in place my chores became lighter and easy to accomplish. The animals were fed in the stable and watered, occasionally wood chopping usually in the company of the elder daughter. We had become quite good buddies. With free time on hand and no school me and my friend roamed the street and especially behind the barns. Looking for adventure, one time we surprised a hawk trying to carry a fat chicken away, chasing him he dropped his prize which we grabbed instantly and brought it to the friend's mother who proceeded to cook it and make a great soup from it, it lasted 2 days.

The mother of my friend was of an unusual character, one I will not forget. Hard as nails and the same time with a great smile on her face that was radiant, confident, and unrelenting belief in life. Just absolutely no apology for any pain or joy she may have given you in a very clear opinion about you or your behavior. At the same time that I was worked for the police/mayor, a work crew from an agriculture school was passing with their wagon from the nearby town to a village past us with a large estate with lots of woods that belonged to the state now to do some wood cutting. The wagon was horse drawn and the students were sitting on each side of the wagon with feet dangling. Axes and hand saws piled between them. One of the students was a cousin to my friend Iwashu. His parents lived in the same village on the opposite end. The students were always singing mostly war inspired songs very moving and I liked them a lot.

One day an axe fell off the wagon and was retrieved by my friend for his family to use. On a visit to exchange some sausage from his father's larder, we obtained some vodka, with very high alcohol content, without his permission. It had to light in a spoon without any warming, trust me it is very powerful. She knew that the sausage was stolen from her brother in law which she accepted without any reservation in exchange for a half pint of very potent whiskey. She then proceeded to preach to us about the axe we found and didn't return it to the rightful owners. We denied any knowledge and swore of our innocence. The reason we were accused is because we were the only ones seen in the streets of their passing and having exchanged greeting to them. The vodka that we obtained we used that weekend to go to a dance at the local school and got drunk and started to pinch some of the girls behinds and on their complaints were thrown out. I better say booted out of the dance into the frigid night tumbling down the street and falling into the ditch. Luckily it was dry. We had a hard time climbing out in our own drunken stupor. Finally we climbed to the street level, to stumble home for a good sleep in the hayloft. I did not get drunk for many years after that experience. Talking of the school of hard knocks, I guess that was one lesson not to be so easily forgotten.

I spent a lot of time in my friend's house watching his father make boots just for everyday work in just two sizes, small and large. Straw and rags made them all fit and warm. They were the color of dark brown and wrinkled, reaching up to your knees. No distinction between women and men, just the size.

In early January 1946, tax officers came through the village on their way home to town and were invited by my boss for drinks and food and with a promise that they would be provided with a ride back to town. After consumption of food and the ever-present vodka, they left on the promised ride to town and were held up after leaving the village and relieved of the money; the driver slightly bruised an innocent bystander. The following morning a group of soldiers arrived on the scene and followed the trail in the snow straight to the hideout. They arrested hold up man gave in quick to the interrogators and my boss was one of the men arrested and thrown in jail.

Chapter 10
Another Resettling

At this time mother received a warning from a visiting police inspector. That inspired her to register for one of the last trains to leave for Poland. So she registered all four of us, the nanny was included again as a distant relative. This time she was a Pole, no problem. While we waited for the last transport to leave for Poland. An election was in progress with lots of resistance from the native Ukrainian and we witnessed truck loads of young people being arrested and hauled away under guard, what a shame. The Russian statement of their high voting participation is in a way true.

My friend's father told us of his adventure on the election day on arriving at his designated voting place was in a school, and when entering the hall he signed the register form and was handed a ballot and was told to drop it in a box across the room. When he tried to open it and take a peek. He was told that committee of communist party had selected the proper candidate for the position. He just went to the other side of the room and after doing his duty in this scam, he went home. The officials took the ballot boxes to the bed-ridden people in homes and hospitals. No wonder their voting percentage is always that high.

Before we left mother sold the wheat that I had received from the Polish people in the form of stalks still growing in the field. I also received a length of home spun and hand woven cloth. Linen, grey of course and my mother made me a pair of work pants from it. A few times that I got them wet they were stiff enough to stand up all by themselves.

Going back to the wheat, mother sold it at the farmers market, with that money she bought a small pig and had it slaughtered and pickled in a wooden tub with a lid to take to our new destination. What a farce of sorts. Because for the last 2 months we lived on boiled potatoes, dry bread, and the occasional onion washed down with water. One thing stands out, in our stay in Russia, we never were really hungry and our food was not very good or bad, just the same as everybody else in that village.

Before we left in the later part of February 1946 for the land of milk and honey and that it was in a sense. On one stop of the train in Neisse we all disembarked and proceeded to father's residence carrying most of our baggage on a hand pulled wagon sent by father, what a change from just less than a year ago we were twice as rich with money and luggage arriving from Russia. Arriving at our new home to be, we were bathed and doused with kerosene to get rid of the lice. To this day I don't know which is worse, the lice or the kerosene.

Next we two young ones were ushered into my father's office sitting down on a table with a big plate full of sugar glazed donuts, a specialty of the bakery, staring and not believing we had to be prompted by father to try some and obliged him hesitantly. For the next few weeks we ate a lot of salt pork and to this day I haven't eaten any again.

We found out from father his adventure after his arrest and release by the Russian commander, that he didn't quit walking till it got dark, seeking a place to stay the night, approached a single standing farmhouse just with 2 women and 2 children residing, he was given a place in the hayloft and some late supper. He stayed a few days and helped them with chores and proceeded down the road, winding up in Krakow, a western Polish town, selling some of the gold coins, obtaining fake identification papers, proceeding to Neisse and opening the bakery. Everything thanks to the good mighty dollar "gold!"

I started helping in the store and bakery, goods were not the only things traded, remember all the Nazi currency covering the tracks of the railroad going to Russia, now we were buying them at a premium, 120 Polish for 100 Nazi money. Times do change. The Nazi money was smuggled into west Germany to be used on the black markets, like cigarette, soup, perfume, just luxury items that were brought back to Poland for the black market.

Father also dealt in jewelry. The Nazi currency and jewelry he sold to a monthly visitor from Krakow who was a Polish army officer. At one time after my arrival father exchanged a 20 gold coin at the state bank for 10,000 slotys no questions asked. He needed extra spending money to satisfy a blackmailer, a rather pleasant and costly situation. The blackmailer, a police inspector and his girlfriend invited father for shopping and club hopping with him paying the bill naturally. I doubt father suffered too much since thinking of himself as a playboy of sorts.

Chapter 11
Our Fourth Resettling

At this time we were a total of 8 people in their extended family. Good and behold for that old cliché "Ethnic cleaning". I really got to like it. In June and July of that year, the Poles began registering and shipping the remaining Germans to the western zones. We took advantage of this and in 3 different groups were sent by the graces of the Polish government to different parts of west Germany.

Sister Helene and me together with mothers iron ration provisions left first and arrived in Bremen. We were then harbored in a small village near Hamburg where we stayed for a few weeks and we were then reunited with mother in northern Bavaria.

The people who harbored us in the village were the most kind and caring human beings that I encountered anywhere.

The reason for us to leave in 3 small groups was, as not to create suspicion because the bakery stayed open to the last day. The easy way that we found all of us in west Germany lays in the fact that we had one central safe house and this consisted of sister Maria's mother in law, that lady lived in central Bavaria and she was the address given to the Red cross. After that in a very short time we were together or at least known where everybody was. One thing I have to say proudly, we Huperts always know how to survive and to recoup. On my arrival in west Germany I developed a "holier than holy" moral attitude for years to come and not to change this conceit until after my arrival in the states.

Now all of us were back in West Germany, the only missing member of the family was Brother Johann, missing in action on the Russian front. Mother's unshakeable belief that he was alive was sometimes depressing and she proved us wrong in years to come.

On our arrival in western Germany, people needed passports to travel between the zones. When we arrived at my mother's camp in Weiden Oberpfalz first we stayed in a large barrack with 3 section of about 40 people with one stove fired by wood and coal for cooking and heat, slept in bunks that were arranged along the walls, one water spigot with a bucket underneath to catch dripping water from the faucet. Outsides latrines, women and men separate, cold water showers for the whole camp of 4 barracks. For cooking we had only cans found at the dump that Americans used. They were the only ones with cans in their daily life. So we had sizes from one gallon to about a quart, all food was boiled, nothing fried or baked. First you had to burn off the olive green paint on the outside of the military cans which created a lot of smoke and bad smell. In time they were faded out through purchase of new pots and pans of a very poor quality. I guess lousy is better than nothing. On one occasion we were issued peanut butter and we were dumbfounded of its use. Some tried to eat it just to have it get stuck on the roof of the mouth. Thanks, no thanks.

On one occasion the American officer in charge of the town gave a speech to the assembled people in the town square arriving in a horse drawn coach and gave us Germans his opinion what was wrong with our lives and that Ammis would show us the right direction to go and to become a democratic thinking people. He was a sorry sight to behold, alcoholic and rambling on without any direction, or believable goals, a very poor representation of the USA. Luckily there were a lot of positive sights to the American presence to make everything good again.

This camp was built on cinder heaps and had housed foreign workers in the war for the glass factory nearby. Arriving in Weiden I encountered my first Americans, mostly M.P.s on motorcycles and in cars. Rations were still in force and also Nazi currency, hungry we were not, thanks to extra ration cards from Sister Maria, who had no use for them. She was married to a man from Bavaria by the name Rudy Seidel, an agriculture expert managing an estate for an absent Baron. He oversaw about 2 dozen people in the farming operation and almost twice as many during harvest time. So food was not a critical item for them which benefitted the extended family.

Mother started to build a small garden on top of the cinders and we fetched mulch. Topsoil from nearby forests and power lines road right of way initially fetched by bucket and then hand pulled wagon, a gift from my brother in law Rudy. That garden became an envy of neighbors and was copied by some. After a year in this camp we were treated to better and more private quarters. The big hall was divided into family units with a table, a couple chairs, and small wood and coal fired stove and 3 double bunks.

In our new quarters we also had an elderly man as an occupant. He smoked the most hideous mixture of tobacco in his pipe. With my mother's constant complaining, he moved out and was replaced by an elderly lady from Prussia. She stayed a few months and was reunited with her family thru the efforts of the Red Cross. The new civil authority came to function with more efficiency than the stupid bureaucrats of the Nazis.

Finally in early 1947 I was able to obtain a much needed surgery to repair my hernia. I had a few close calls by not wearing my makeshift belt and that was not a very nice experience with my gut hanging out and retreating after time back into my belly cavity. This led to quite a few moments of anxiety. The surgery was performed in the city hospital where the nursing staff consisted of catholic nuns, what great human beings. They made my stay a more pleasant experience. Thank God for that.

The same year I was confirmed and having arrived at the church without a sponsor, I approached a middle aged gentleman outside of the church and he agreed to be my sponsor. He was a refugee from Selesia still looking for his family. The sermon during the service was by a Jesuit priest. It made an unforgettable impression and set a code of conduct for me for the rest of my life. He gave us a sample of absolute justice. It was as follows. If you borrowed 25 cents on Thursday and promised to pay it back at Friday at noon, then on 12 noon, not a minute less or more, not a penny less or more. That was absolute justice. Anything else is tempered by kindness or any other abrasion and is not perfect justice. This sermon made me what I am as a person today trying my best to achieve justice as best as possible.

While attending the last year of school for me, 6th grade to be exact, which I finished with straight A's, a remarkable thing happened to me, I suddenly was able to understand everything in the class and without any doubts. Next stage in my life was to learn a trade because higher schooling was of question for two reasons, having lost 2 years from my education and the other no money. I entered an apprenticeship in an automotive repair shop. At that time I had 6 weeks to make up my mind to stay or not to stay; the same for the employer. If it was agreed to by both parties then the contract could not be broken easily for the time of the apprenticeship, 3-4 years. I made great strides and was quick to catch on and also accepted in that shop of about 8 employees. The special benefits given by the employer since ration cards were still in use.

Lots of the repairs were paid with goods, especially the butchers and also the baker. Our boss treated the shop to two snacks a day; cold cuts, cheese, and various breads. He sure changed my opinion about the Reichsdeutche. I did not complain after 6 weeks for the reason that there was no soap on the job or in our daily life, and no rubber aprons. The cleaning of motor parts in kerosene with brushes was very dirty and penetrated my clothes to the skin, no scrubbing with lava stone soap could get it out. So I quit that apprenticeship.

I became an apprentice in a cabinet mill workshop, what my mother had found in a very short time after my try of auto mechanics. I never dreamed of such a thing, electronics were my passion. My boss was a very reserved man on the dry side. I did surprise him with my born engineering ability. On an installation project with him, very early into my employment, I would hand him tools or supplies before he even asked for them. The first time it happened he called out, how did you know that, I just did.

After one year I started doing small jobs in the camp from scrap wood. Book cases and in one instance in a small wardrobe from hard maple, scrounged from the railroad yard. Everything by hand. A short time later my father surprised me with a set of brand new woodworking tools and tried to talk me into quitting my apprenticeship and going into the furniture repair business, but I declined.

Meanwhile we had another change coming, we were transferred to a more spacious camp on the outskirts of town. When we moved to our new larger quarters in the new location we had two large rooms plus a storage area in a separate building. My mother and I built a chicken coop with an outdoor pen fenced in. Mother obtained ½ dozen young laying hens and suddenly I saw eggs for my breakfast, what a life. After a while the eggs disappeared and with it some of my mother's baking when asking what happened to the eggs or the lack of them created a funny situation between me and mother. When questioning her about my missing breakfast fare, I was told that a young woman in the camp would come for them, so that way there were never any for me. Asking her about how much she charged the woman for said eggs, I was told to my astonishment nothing, when asked why, she said that the woman was pregnant and you could not refuse a pregnant woman her wish because if you did, the mice would eat your crops. Every time I remember that episode I have to break out in laughter.

The Americans sponsored a boys club in the town with different activities. One was boxing which I took for about one year. I had lots of fun, just couldn't keep up with too much demand on my time. I was working 48 hrs a week; plus cleaning the shop on 5 days of the week for half an hour or more and for 4 hours on Saturday. Not to mention the one hour walk to and from work to my home.

Finally the day arrived of new currency, no border between the western zones and ration cards became history. Suddenly overnight goods appeared like by a miracle in the show windows, shiny bicycles, stylish clothes and goodies we only dreamed of like bananas, oranges, and even café like establishments serving primarily coca cola and a few snacks. Life began to look up for everybody. The tempo of everyday life picked up especially in this small town with no visible war damage to dampen your spirits.

At this time Helene mother and I were living in the new camp, Sister Helene graduated from school and went to live with older sister Maria in Gut Weng with her husband and 3 children in a small place with about 6 farms. father sometimes showed up, mostly he was like a rolling stone residing all over western Germany and I guess enjoying himself. My oldest sister Anni's husband returned home from the USA in 1947 where he was interned in a prison camp in Clinton Maryland. Just 15 miles from the capital which he got to see quite often on detail.

Life continued at its new paces and was quite enjoyable. Then in early 1948 we received the news that brother Johann was alive as a German prisoner of war in Russia. mother was ecstatic and started to make plans for his arrival. We received few letters from him, about 3 in one year and then miracle of miracles in December 1950 he arrived home just in time for mother's birthday what a time. He brought a few new things with him that I have never seen, instant coffee- you just add hot water and voila coffee was ready, cream and sugar already there. Pants from Japan were lined in the knee area with silk fabric so as not to stick to your shin while bending or crawling.

Primitive locks made by the prisoners to sell to the Russian civilian was permitted by the soviets. In one of the get togethers of the whole family while discussing all the tribulation that befell on us, one thing stood out, we were never physically or verbally abused, what speaks a lot about people in this world, enemies and friends alike. Family is something else. Sister Hedy immigrated to the USA to marry a German born American. he lived in

Baden Prince George county, Maryland, 25 miles from the capitol, Washington D.C. In a short time less than 6 months, brother Johann moved away to get married to the sister of one of his friends from the prison camp in Russia.

Before he left to his new life he told us of his adventure in the army and the following prisoner of war experience. He was a truck driver, first Ammo and he drove a Studebaker, captured in Dunkirk. That truck was blown up by a bomb, hit and he wound up driving a field kitchen vehicle till his capture by the Russians. His army group got surrounded by the Russians in 1944 and he spent 4 months behind Russian lines having obtained civilian clothes and portraying himself as a Polish forced laborer working in the German supply lines. He was eventually found out and sent to a prisoner of war camp. Because of his knowledge of 4 languages he was made a leader of a road and small construction brigade, thanks to fellow prisoners who were engineers he was able to fulfill this position. He also was entrusted by the camp commander to go under guard on bi-weekly occasion to sell gadgets that the prisoners made, things like locks, kitchen knives, and other very much needed items by the Russian public in return he bought eggs, bread, potatoes, and lots of other products in quantities that required him to hire a farmer with a horse wagon to bring it all back to camp.

On the question of escape he told us the following story: Half a dozen prisoners escaped and were recaptured by the sergeant of the guard and returned to the camp in a flat bed truck, just to be buried because they were all dead. Shot by the sergeant who would have no more of anybody trying the same stunt.

Sister Rosa moved into town and worked as a live in maid and as a photo studio helper in Weiden. We had lots of fun together. one of my friends from work immigrated to Canada with his family and was encouraging me to follow what I considered to do.

Chapter 12
Off to the USA

Telling this to my sister Hedy in America, she suggested coming to the USA. Her husband would sponsor me and guarantee employment. The red tape delays and bureaucratic shenanigans took at least 8 months of processing before receiving the green light to enter the USA. The same was accomplished in 5 weeks to go to Canada.

After saying goodbye to my family and never to see mother again I proceeded to camp in Dachau then by train with other hopefuls to Breman for final embarkment onto a ship to the USA. travelling by ship, a former military transport in the first weeks of December 1951 was quite an adventure, the North Atlantic is not known for its calmness in that part of the year. Half of my 10 day trip was spent sick in my berth, which was located right above the screw and each time the ship crested a wave and came crashing down, was a total nerve destroying happening.

I arrived in New York on the 13th of December 1951 in the evening, the next day I moved for a one night stay to a camp in town and then left on a plane to Washington, DC. First time flying, not bad. My sister and her husband John Pirner received me at the airport about 10 pm and at greeting them I learned that greeting a man in the USA was not to hug and kiss him on the lips Galizian style, no-no, not accepted in this worldly society, we do learn don't we after this debacle.

We proceeded to their home in the darkness for about 30 miles, half of it on an oiled gravel road seeing nothing except a few houses still with lights on arriving on the farm late we went to sleep to awaken in my new world. Finding out to my sorrow German was spoken only since there was no need for English, all residents in the house were German. Sister Hedy , John, and his elderly father, the father being in the states since 1913 spoke only the most rudiment English barely making it.

I learned in a short time to milk cows, digging stumps out by hand and no matter how I searched and bent over, no gold was on the streets. My sister's concern for my security and welfare was a scam just to obtain reliable help for the farm. My pay was fair except for late in coming, one year and

7 months late. Before that I made little money from a vegetable garden, helping in old grandpa's sawmill. I was just 19 years old with no care and enjoyed myself with what was on this place. Just as luck would have it there was a complete collection of books about the rise of Western civilization and guess what, in German. Somebody had given these books to the old man and he deposited them in the attic of a lean on and never to turn a page.

Attending mass at St. Peters church I discovered to my surprise how over dressed I was and stuck out like a sore thumb. The girls and their mamas liked my appearance, with no money or wheels I couldn't capitalize on that fact. With my first real money in hand I bought a Hudson commodore, navy blue , a great road hugging machine.. now that I was able to move about, move I did, mostly to my sister's in-laws house with 4 boys and one girl all about my age. This family owned a T.V. and a telephone. I would watch TV from this only English speaking residence, their native language-guess what, "English".

I also encountered many new things and never seen or used before never fazed me a bit, just approved it as something natural to use without hesitation. This very modern family were Jehovah witnesses and they tried their damndest to convert me, little did they know that I had enough propaganda of any kind and had developed a very thick skin, to this day I hate to wear any logos on my clothes or bumper stickers on my vehicle. All the badgering and trying to save my soul from everlasting damnation was wasted on me. I do owe this family a lot of gratitude.

The house that my sister and her family lived in was started by my brother in law in 1939 and never to be finished till after my arrival. He was building this house for his future wife, a neighbor's daughter and when her parents discovered that relationship it ended. With a good spanking and almost locking her up, they had a dire need for her on the farm for babysitting and a lifetime maid, poor thing died a spinster. her parents had no remorse just an arrogant attitude of righteousness.

On the abrupt break up of this relationship, brother in law quit working on the house till the arrival of my sister Hedy. They lived in an old salt box house, until he got the new house liveable. On my arrival there were still 2 rooms unfinished and about half the exterior siding was still missing. In less than a year we finished this project except the back porch.

Meanwhile my sister Rosa also arrived from Germany and stopped over by us on her way to Florida to a family where she was committed to them having sponsored her entry into the USA, so now we were 3 siblings in America and were talking about bringing over Sister Maria over. After her husband had died in January 1952, nothing came of it and Maria was able to take over the management of the estate where she was very successful and retired from it somewhere in 1980.

Slowly I began to tear down all the lean-ons and other delapidated buildings on the property. That job was not totally accomplished until 7 yrs later. Brother in law was a very meticulous person, self taught in many trades, carpentry, plumbing, electrician, masonry, and concrete work everything done in a very high craftsmanship manner, the only drawback, just very slow. He built stables and one tobacco curing barn with jointery to make many professional master carpenters jealous.

Their same standard was applied also to tobacco raising, with very good results on auction day. We were rewarded with top dollar for our efforts. he was a short man of about 5 foot 3 inches, tough as nails, very well read and I liked him a lot. Grandfather hated tobacco and never raised it and so lost out on a labor rewarding cash crop in this region. He dabbled with a gristmill, sawmill and eggs production, everything on a small scale and never to become much of a success.

With the car I became more adventurous. I took a trip to New York and visited with my sister Rosa who lived in Newark, New Jersey. She took me to an Italian restaurant, we had a great pizza, a first for me; a very enjoyable trip with the car also arose a greater need for money so I found employment for the slow months, late fall and winter in a cabinet shop run by an English man by the name of Henry

Key. He was a newcomer from London, England. I learned a lot from him and worked in that shop for the next two winters. Come spring back to farming and the outdoors which I enjoyed tremendously.

I traded in my Hudson for more of an American icon "a pickup", a Ford 150 to be exact with a rear bumper and a heater which was extra. Unwittingly I became more and more of an American, blue jeans, T-shirt and loafers almost daily attire. Celebrating thanksgiving and fourth of July parade, not to mention the fireworks in Washington D.C. On my third thanksgiving in the USA I experienced the unusual appearance of the smallest turkey ever. In the morning of that day a quail flew into the window screen and was killed. I went outside and found the bird and roasted it just like a turkey, the most beautiful midget turkey you ever saw. Showed the beauty to some friends of mine and their parents. Eating the full-size turkey was a better choice.

I started to date, drive in movies, fishing on the bay and the reason of a back seat of a car. Living the American dream to the fullest with just one dark cloud hanging over my head. I am not very knowledgeable of clouds except this one was not easy to forget, "draft board". While living on the farm I began to meet and interact with colored people on a personal basis. Some were neighbors, other occasional help needed during the harvest of the tobacco. I just couldn't understand the double standard and discrimination in the American society. It bothered me a lot especially seeing it in the household I lived in, with my sister- the worst. This hypocrisy was very offensive to me, especially when I was looked on like some sort of weirdo in this respect, some of the black people were also confused by my attitude.

Chapter 13
I Join the US Army

With the draft board persistence, and not able to be deferred. I volunteered with the option to enlist for the anti aircraft missile control and was accepted on fulfillment of the necessary qualifications and joined the army for 3 years. That missile control was a 58 week course in electronics which was the passion and dream of my youth, not to mention a great future would await me back in the civilian world after my enlistment. Little did I know of the army's ways. While in 8 weeks of training in fort Jackson South Carolina, the qualification for that schooling were changed and I became disqualified to attend. All of this was unknown to me while going through the first 8 weeks of training.

While in basic training, I enjoyed my duties in the kitchen and also the service line, these duties that kept me from a lot of nit-picking crap dished out by want to be Napoleons. My personal uniforms were all tailored and adjusted for the perfect fit. My bed was always made, shoes Polished, I drove the NCO's crazy, they needed something to find wrong with us recruits.

My broken English came always to my rescue. I would get excited and start cussing in a mix of German and English. They learned to leave me alone and pick on somebody else. I think it also helped by being 23 and not like most recruits who were just 18. For that matter I have already experienced this world much better than most NCO's who were mostly no older than myself. My favorite job on K.P. was pots and pans. That was one place where nobody bothered you, not even the cooks. Being on K.P. or on duty on the serving line, gave me access to the pantry with all its goodies which I obtained quite liberally and shared with my comrades in the field while training. I made a lot of friends that way.

While in the first 8 weeks of training with Christmas approaching we had a Christmas drive for needy military children, who we took for a tour of shopping and rewarded with a weekend pass in the town of Columbia. My charge a little girl who had $18 to spend and typical of a future woman, spent twice as much which came out of my pocket. I didn't mind at all, it was a later fun, and never to be forgotten. Later that day my friends and fellow elves went to a great dinner in a restaurant where I ate for the first time, a great steak with all the trimmings. What a memory.

As you can see not everything bad, some very memorable moments did occur and what I treasure to this day. After finishing the training and being denied the promise made by the recruiter, I was sent to Fort Eustis Virginia. At my departure from Fort Jackson, I had my pick up stored off the post for a monthly fee, I was joined by 2 fellow recruits, one from Maryland, and the second from Maine whom I dropped off at the bus station in D.C. I was approached by two Black recruits from N.C. to give them a ride in back of the pickup, which I agreed to do. Stopping at a road stand, getting some trinkets and food in my Broken English, witnessing a very upsetting scene, the Black soldiers were refused service for food and told to go to the side door. This injustice bothered me a lot and took the desire to become a citizen of this country right out of me. I, a son of a Nazi and former Hitler Youth member with scant English got service, and the sons more likely of American Veterans did not.

What a rude awakening from all the propaganda that was dished out to us in post war Germany by hot air spewing Amis. While in Fort Eustis I tried one more time to get my enlistment promise fulfilled and wound up in fort Sill, Oklahoma in a school for ground to ground missiles, which only officer rank personal could attend.

After a few more weeks of military fumbling I arrived in fort bliss Texas and after a few weeks with new classes forming I finally have arrived. How foolish of me to think so, after 5 weeks basic electronic and before entering the missile secrest component section,I was booted out of class, because not being a citizen yet.

Appealing to the inspector General's office, I appeared before the officers in charge. And complaining about the unfairness of the situation because the same time they were sending no American citizens Nato Troops by droves to the same class. Their excuse was that they were friends of the USA. "What short memory we have." What a crock, this officer sure lowered my opinion about officers and gentlemen. I was told that I had to have advanced training before attending that class. A lie.

I was sent to anti aircraft artillery training on twin 40mm cannons on a tank chassis and quadruple 50 caliber machine guns mounted on a halftrack. Lots of fun. I spent some time in the Texan desert quite an adventure. On one of the maneuvers in the desert for about a week we were surprised after evening discharge to hear bells ringing, what a surprise and welcome sight of a good humor ice cream truck to show up, I treated the group of soldiers that I belonged to an ice cream bar. For some reason nobody had any money including the lieutenant of our platoon except me. I offered one to the platoon leader a lieutenant who refused it with a salivating mouth I'm sure. He would not accept my offer of an ice cream bar and had to watch us enjoying our treat.

Finishing my advanced training, I returned, to the frustration of the command of the whole regiment to attend the classes, just to be told it will not happen. In November 1956 I got married to a Mexican girl by the name Irene Nava who was living with her married sister in the USA. When I announced my intention to get married to the "black Bismarck" a master sergeant took me under his wings. He warned me that marrying a Mexican in Texas was the same as marrying a black girl in the south at that time. In my youthful exuberance and being in love, I just laughed and went ahead and got married in El Paso Texas on November 1956 which I never regretted. At that time I was in the service over a year and still only a private not assigned only attached with no chance of promotion.

I got married again on the 6th of January 1957 in Mexico in the church. Going on a honeymoon trip to Maryland, we went to see the senator of our district who arranged an appointment at the general inspector's office at the pentagon. I was told that there would be waiting an assignment and belated rank for me on the return to the regiment. That was true, on my return I was assigned to a brigade supply room with the rank of specialized second class. That action restored some of my faith to officers and gentlemen. In a short time I became a father of a beautiful girl that we named Juliet Diane Hupert born in the great state of "Texas". She got a certificate and permission to wear a ten gallon hat.

One funny thing happened to my wife on one of her visits to the base doctor. He asked her what part of Germany she was from, she shocked him by telling him she was Mexican and learned most of her English from her German husband. From my wife's family I learned a lot about Mexican peasant's lives. Their ambition and desire are the same as any other person I met, everybody striving to forge ahead and improve their lives in a strong surge for betterment. Superstitions and the dos and don'ts of religion casting a shadow on their endeavors.

Chapter 13
Back to Civilian Life

Prior to my discharge in 1958, two months ahead of time, I took my small family and belongings, loaded into my old Oldsmobile after disengaging the back seat to make room for what little we had and took off for Maryland to my sister's place to spend my 30 days of leave and finishing to take down dilapidated buildings including the old salt box house. old grandpa had died the previous year and in his place found my father visiting for 6 months from Germany, what a pleasant surprise. He got to meet my family which he really appreciated.

At the end of my furlough I returned to Fort Bliss and awaited my discharge in 30 days. My wife and daughter stayed in Maryland waiting for my return, which I did promptly. We moved into an apartment with lots of young families and small children. I went to work for Mr. Henry Key again and found out that Mr.Key was a very lousy business man and was going down the tube. I started to look for better employment, what I found in a short time through an interior design friend.

This friend Jimmy Kiefer was from Philadelphia with a mind of genius. Any detail in furniture making, telephone numbers, or street address would stay in his mind forever, he never entered it in any form into a ledger or rolodex, no matter where or what, Hong Kong, Italy, or Greece. Not to mention first class gourmet cook was another of his talents, which I and my partner got to enjoy a few times.

I started to work for Mr. Pierre Bartet a French man. This shop was very prestigious and I learned a lot and gained experience in fine furniture making, what came to very good use in my future. This Frenchman was planning to go into manufacturing for high quality goods and I started to look for new employment because factory flooring was not for me. After two more tries to work for somebody else I decided after a couple months to open my own business. What I did with a small loan from a bank and help from a friend, an Englishman named David Feldman who was an interior designer, he promptly started sending jobs to me and he also encouraged his friend in his guild to use me. The gratitude that I owed this man and his wife is immense just to have their opinion of me spoiled by my ex partner and so called "friend". He told that man of some anti semantic statements that I supposedly had made about him which was a total lie. Some people are hard to understand. This partner of mine wouldn't be where he is today without my presence in his life.

I had done commercials, exibitions, and private residence work. I took on a partner Joseph Klapal, a Cech born cabinet maker my age and with him we progressed in a very short time to be the premier shop for years to come in the Washington D.C. area.

I and my wife had three more children, Adam Oscar, Irene Katharina, and Stanley Joseph, very great kids and a lot of fun. Acquiring our first house which I immediately enlarged and improved. Again the residents in this subdivision were mostly young people, working for the government or in the private sector and few self employed like me. My wife made a lot of friends and introduced me to them, she was the force in our social life and I tagged along for lots of fun and friendship. I guess I was living the American dream, wife, kids, house, pet, and do not forget a lawnmower to fill the house of plenty.

One of my private customers took a liking to me and invited me on a charter fishing trip in the bay, what an experience and a new avenue to relax, enjoy and not to mention some great eating. My wife was a very good cook and would not hesitate to try new things, sometimes I helped out especially on big gatherings. From tacos, pierogies, sauerbraten, grilled steaks and the ever American dish, hamburgers. These dishes were a routine in our house and appreciated by friends and family alike.

I built my own boat that was shared by my friends and neighbors alike, what was a lot of fun. On a visit to my friend's parents in the country, me and my wife were persuaded after 18 years in this country to try the great Maryland delicatessen steamed crab. I never lost the taste for them, only it has to be eaten in Maryland.

In 1966 with business doing great my partner and me purchased a 100 acre farm with gulley and a stream fed by a spring. The previous owner had quit farming because of age and had built himself a small house on a 1 acre lot on the edge of this farm. I befriended him in time and received a lot of information from him about this area. The farm had a barn, old 2 story salt box house with indoor plumbing, detached garage and small smoke and meat shed. We utilized the farm for outings with overnight stays in the old house. On purchasing a used farm tractor with attachments. I kept the fields open and clear. The bush hogging and clearing the underbrush exposed me to the outdoors, not to mention the straw hat and striped overalls that gave me lots of satisfaction and peace of mind.

We built a 5 acre pond and stocked it with fish, now swimming, fishing and ice skating were added fun to owning the farm and enjoyed by family and friends. I almost forgot dirt bike riding and hunting which provided some great meals on our table.

in 1969 we moved to a subdivision in Port Tobacco Charles Country Maryland, just 2 miles from the farm. That move was a great happening for our school age children, there were no fences on the large and level lots, where the kids used to play, from one end to the other like roaming bandits. Now I had to upgrade my lawnmower, the push would not do to cut almost 2 acres of grass.

I was invited to join the local Lion 's Club and that I did, the same time proceeding to become a USA citizen. A short time after swearing in as a citizen, my wife gave me a big surprise party and fellow Lion Club members presented me with a flag which flew over the capital. I still own this flag, slightly tattered I take it out only to show it to visitors and back into the drawer it goes. The change of mind to become a citizen was brought on by a large degree to the fact that the country was slowly striving for equality and made positive steps in that direction. Having witnessed the good of the people. In general, I arrived at the conclusion to join my wife and children to be one of the countless masses of this great country.

Life was very satisfying not much of a challenge, which was to change in the near future. I became frustrated to be stuck in the groove of nothingness and security of my well being. On my partner's urgency we built a shop on the farm big enough for 5 people to work in. I became more and more disillusioned and started to think about a break from the partnership with the idea to go into the construction business.

I eventually did in 1972 with all of our 4 kids in school my wife became restless and talked me into opening a sandwich shop in a office building in nearby Waldorf for her to run and to occupy herself and to make spending money. Unfortunately she could not handle the pressure and I was obligated to run it by myself. After a year or less we were able to sell this business at cost and I went back full-time into construction. I was trying to develop a small plot of 8 acres with 4 building lots on it.

I approached the bank for construction loans which was favorably looked on with the stipulation that I had to get my sister to subrogate a loan from her on the property which she agreed to do. After paying the bank an earnest deposit and prepping the lots for construction, incurring latter expenses, and being notified by the bank of the approval of the loan, I disengaged myself from a contract to build a custom home for a client in preparation for building on my lots. Notifying my sister of this fact we will have a settlement on a given date which she agreed to, just to call a few days later that she will not subrogate her loan to the bank. nothing in the world could persuade her to change her mind.

Overnight I wound up losing thousands of dollars, hard earned money and worse, no job. Did I say she was mean born. Unknown to me I went into some kind of depression for the next few years and struggled to survive.

After the lunch room debacle my wife and me became foster parents at her urging. She was very good with children and very attentive to her charges. In short time we wound up with a 2 day old boy infant that my wife named Joey. After a few month stay he was returned to social services to my wife's heartbreak. The second, also an infant boy 2 days old who was promptly named Peter, because he arrived in the house shortly before Easter. "Peter Rabbit". This explanation is for the people a little slow in the thinking department.

The social service had a hard time to obtain relief for the adoption to go forward, after 12 months they approached us to see if we wanted to adopt this child that the family already was treating like one of us. The resounding yes that they received the very next day must have caused a little disturbance in the offices of the social services. Within 3 months or less the court in La Plata, Maryland awarded us the toddler with his golden locks and 2 different colored eyes. We arranged for a belated baptism and named him Peter Adam Hupert, what a great son and human being. That I am proud of him like all of my kids, 8 in all. No preference or dislike for any of them in case you wonder, eight kids I will explain.
My marriage deteriorated in the near future and we were divorced in 1978. The blame for that failure is hard to assign. I will willingly accept the guilt for it, I am still friends with my ex.

In 1980 I started my own cabinet business again with the help of my oldest son Adam Oscar who would be followed soon by his brother Stanley Joseph. The same year I met my future wife to be on a blind date for dinner in a restaurant arranged by my niece Janie who was my date's car pool member. She was a divorcee with two girls 5-6 years old, adorable characters and "characters they were", Megan and Colleen and I have loved them ever since.

I got married to Patricia T. Maloney on the 19th of February 1982 and have been happy ever since. With the marriage I wound up cutting grass again slightly demoted, it only took 50 feet of extension cord and small electric motor driven thing. I was involved in the cabinet business, construction till my retirement in 1994. In 1985 on 11th of November we were blessed by a little girl we named Monica Louise Hupert.

And now you have the explanation of all 8 children. In my fleeting years I was engaged by a private customer. The types dreams are made of, a real Renaissance self made couple with two kids, with great taste and with genuine kindness and grace. They were really fun to work for.

My wife had taken an early retirement offer by the Postal Service where she was employed in the administration section and started to build a new career in the "real estate" industry. In May of 1994 we moved south to the North Carolina coast to the island of Oak Island in the southernmost county of Brunswick in N.C.

We enrolled our daughter in the much maligned and chastisized NC school system. Schooling is a partnership between parents and schools. What lots of people seem to forget and then try to blame the failure of their kids onto the poor teacher. It was a very wonderful experience for our sunshine born daughter. My wife resumed the real estate and I continued to dabble in cabinet making with great neighbors of all kinds, my favorite the southern folks. Taking a break from my cabinet making and enjoying some of my pastry and coffee gazing out of the window, what do I see:" Kukoraciak."

1951
Refugee Camp at
Weiden Oberpfalz, Bavaria

Katharina Hupert,
Author's Mother

Adam, Mother, and sister, Rosa

Poem written by Rosa Hupert, Adam's Sister

EPIC POEM

At around the year seventeen thirty five,
East our fore-fathers went,
To follow the call of Catherine the Great,
To settle in a foreign land.

Come one, come all,
Was the battle cry,
So, they go en masse,
No one questions why.

Freedom. Land, Bread and Butter,
For every man, woman and child,
That was the promise from far away Russia,
So, off they go, to yonder wild.

They harnessed their horses to the wagons,
In a great big hurry and little thought,
Their meager belongings tightly packed,
What sort of fate is being wrought ?.

And so, with courage and Holy Bible.
With banners blowing in the wind,
Great expectations and excitement,
Will no one in the group rescind?

On the way now for some time,
Their hopes already much depressed,
Homeless and totally on their own,
The group is losing all its zest.

The children's cries can oft be heard,
The women don't know how to cope,
Why did we leave ? Why did we go ?
Little by little, they're losing hope.

The first fatality after two months,
The new land still far from sight,
The dead are buried along the road,
Dark the future, where's the light?

They traveled for months marked by births and deaths,
Suffered much, toward what end?
Totally exhausted, hardly able to move,
They arrived at last in the "Promised Land".

Hupert-Lempert-Roth and Kammer,
Unloaded their belongings,
With saw and nails and a hammer,
Started to built their humble dwellings.

        Two cows, one calf, (born on the way)
        One horse, (the other to hunger lost),
        Two pigs, some seeds and little longing,
        A new life started on the outpost.

First a roof over the head,
out of stone, straw and clay,
A little village comes to be,
Ebenau it's name, located along Lembergs by-way.

        They built a barn for the lifestock,
        Put seeds into the ground,
        They built a school and a bell tower,
        Thanking God for new home found.

Slow but steady they got ahead,
Found stability, prosperity and joy,
The village and their hopes expanded,
Fate that no one can destroy.

        Of course it was not meant to be,
        The first World War has started,
        They leave their lifestock and homesteads,
        And turn toward Austria half-hearted.

The menfolk serve in the military,
Must defend the Fatherland,
To the women, children and old folks,
Vienna lends a helping hand.

        As the war was nearing end,
        Toward their homes they went,
        The lifestock gone, the field are bare,
        The houses damaged, what punishment.

The danger of war not totally over,
The hand-granades exploding,
People search for a save shelter,
In the air a strange fore-boding.

108

The noise of war-fare is getting louder,
Explosions hitting closer still,
A choking smell envelopes the village,
They cover their faces, all feel ill.

Our Mother with her first two children,
Was hiding in a cellar,
The poison gas killed the little ones,
It was 1918 on the calendar.

Mother has told us many times,
The story of that night,
When she did so with tears unchecked,
We all were full of fright.

But, life went on, the men came home,
once again a new beginning,
Eight children more to Mother born,
Life's challenges they are winning.

But, fate again deals a cruel blow,
Second World War we see erupt,
What will now happen to us all,
What hopes, what dreams disrupt?

Bombs, Russians - "Amis" Hitler,
Heaven has no compassion,
Even hell can-not be worse,
We're drained of all emmotion.

Like through a miracle, even this war,
Has come to a mercifull conclusion,
The family scattered all over Europe,
And left without illusion.

We see the wasteland all around,
No strenght to fight nor die,
Where is everyone, alive or dead?
We search, while years go by.

Finally, against all odds,
Together we all come,
Impoverished, like all D. P's. ,
We start to built a home.

109

What happened to us all since than?
Where did we all end up?
I want to put it down for you,
Now, that you're all grown up.

Grandpa and Grandma,
The war did not survive,
The misery too much for them,
Died, of all comfort deprived.

Mother left us much too early,
Died in nineteen fifty nine,
Life was seldom easy for her,
I love her so, her star will shine.

Father reached advanced age,
Died in nineteen seventy seven,
I say a prayer for him oft,
Hope, he found his place in heaven.

Anne has two sons and a daughter,
Lives in Bavaria, Germany,
Has a nice home and a big garden,
Plus five grandchildren for company.

Johann died much too soon,
I wish he could be with us still,
He had two children, lived near Cologne,
Whenever I think of him, I get a chill!

Maria was the first to marry,
Has six daughters and two sons,
Resides near Munich, Bavaria,
A life full of upheavals and carry-on

Hedy migratet to America,
Near the Capitol a home she found,
She has four daughters and three sons,
Her house stands against a farm background.

Rosa, is also in the States,
My home is in Chicago,
I have two daughters and a son,
Found harmony and peace years ago.

Joseph stayed in Germany,
Lonely, the best years gone by,
Searched for solace in the bottle,
Found nothing else, his life awry.

Adam, on this side of the ocean,
Has eight children at last count,
The east coast also his address,
Many obstacles he had to surmount.

Helene, the youngest lives in Germany,
Has five children and a big farm,
Loves her work and family,
Is very witty, has lots of charm.

And so my loved ones ,
The story is told,
It took me forever,
I am getting old.

I hope you read it once in a while,
I was trying to give you a life's profile.

Dedicated to my children,

Linda Christine, Alfred Joseph and
Elizabeth Marie.

Also to my nieces and nephews,

love Mom
and aunt

by:
Rosa Meixner
Chicago, Illinois

Pencil Sketch of Ebenau Residents

Nationalities of Residents by Lot Numbers

1. German	11. Polish	21. Ukrainian
2. Ukrainian	12. German	22. Polish
3. German	13. Ukrainian	23. German
4. Polish	14. German	24. Russian
5. German	15. German	25. Polish
6. Polish	16. German	26. Ukrainian
7. German	17. Polish	27. Polish
8. Ukrainian	18. German	28. Polish
9. Polish	19. German	29. Ukrainian
19. German	20. Polish	